The
Happy Day® Books
Family Treasury

Presented to

Autumn

Schultz

by

Mrs. Buhler

on

December 23, 2007

The
Happy Day® Books
Family Treasury

50 Popular Stories

Standard
PUBLISHING
Bringing The Word to Life™

Cincinnati, Ohio

ISBN 0-7847-1545-9

11 10 09 08 07 06 05   9 8 7 6 5 4 3 2 1

Introduction

Over the past 25 years, millions of children and their parents have read and enjoyed Happy Day® Books from Standard Publishing. More than 10 million Happy Day® Books have been sold. Now 50 favorite Happy Day® stories are presented together in one wonderful volume to be treasured for years to come!

Explore God's world with Heno Head, Jr., and other writers and encounter many facets of creation—from puppy dogs to dinosaurs, from ocean depths to outer space—in **Stories About God's World.** Experience Bible times in **Bible Stories** as you live on the ark with Noah, travel with Jonah to Nineveh, search for the little lost sheep, and eat breakfast with Jesus.

You'll make knowing God more real—by playing with mom or talking with grandma, singing favorite songs or learning what makes you special—in **Stories About Faith and Family.** Children with strong character will become role models for your family as they learn to work hard, eat wisely, be truthful, and make friends in **Stories About Values.** And don't forget holidays! **Stories About Holidays** help children honor God in your family's holiday celebrations.

The Happy Day® Books Family Treasury is a book for every young family and a book you'll come back to again and again, extending the wonderful influence of Christian books for children to a new generation.

Stories About
God's World

Bible Stories

Stories About
Values

Stories About
Holidays

Stories About
God's World

God the Creator Thought of It First!

written by JOAN N. KEENER

illustrated by
STEPHEN CARPENTER

Our world is full of fun and helpful things made from materials like wood, metal, plastic, and cloth.

Each one began with an *idea*. God has the *best* ideas. In the beginning God made the heavens and the earth—out of *nothing!*

Yes, our world is full of things that began as good ideas . . . but GOD is the one who thought of them first!

A **helicopter** on a rescue mission flies up and down, backward and forward, and hovers in the air. But GOD the creator thought of it first!

God created the . . . **HUMMINGBIRD.** His wings beat *fast* and cause a humming sound. Hummingbirds can fly up and down, backward and forward, and they can hover in the air.

A **submarine** has special tanks that fill with water to make the sub sink. When the water is pumped out of the tanks, the sub rises.

But GOD the creator thought of it first!

God created the . . . **CHAMBERED NAUTILUS.** The bones of this sea creature form small "rooms," or chambers. The chambers empty or fill with water to make the little nautilus go up or down.

To walk over soft, deep snow without sinking, you can wear **snowshoes.** And **snow boots** keep your feet warm. But GOD the creator thought of it first!

He made the . . . **SNOWSHOE RABBIT.** His wide feet keep him on top of the snow. Long hairs grow on the sides of his feet and between his toes. The hairs help the rabbit's feet stay warm.

When you swim underwater, you can breathe with a **snorkel.** But GOD the creator thought of it first!

He made the . . . **ELEPHANT.** He breathes through his trunk when he goes swimming!

When you ride your bike or roller-skate, you wear a **helmet** and **kneepads** for protection. But GOD the creator thought of it first!

God created the . . . **ARMADILLO.** Hard plates protect this creature's body. The plates are jointed so that he can roll up in a ball for extra safety.

If you want to hang a sun catcher in a window, you use a **suction cup.** But GOD the creator thought of it first!

God made the . . . **OCTOPUS.** Two rows of suction cups on each arm help the octopus to stick tight to anything.

When you travel in a **camper,** you are taking your home with you. But GOD the creator thought of it first!

God made the . . . **TURTLE.** His movable home is his shell. He takes it with him wherever he goes, and sometimes he stays inside all day!

A **baby carrier** lets parents keep their babies with them wherever they go. But GOD the creator thought of it first!

God made the . . . **KANGAROO.** A mother kangaroo keeps her baby, called a joey, in a pouch on the front of her body. She takes the little joey with her wherever she goes.

Suspended underneath long "wings" made of cloth, the pilot of a **hang glider** flies from place to place. But GOD the creator thought of it first!

God made the . . . **FLYING SQUIRREL.** To glide from tree to tree, he spreads out the folds of his skin between his front and back legs.

A jumbo jet airplane is pushed through the sky by its huge **jet-propelled engines.** But GOD the creator thought of it first!

God made the . . . **GIANT SQUID.** To move through the ocean, he takes water into a special part of his body and then forcefully jets it out.

Remember, our world is full of things that began as ideas, but . . . GOD is the one who thought of them first!

Ask the animals, and they will teach you. Or ask the birds of the air, and they will tell you. Speak to the earth, and it will teach you. Or let the fish of the sea tell you. Every one of these knows that the hand of the Lord has done this. —*Job 12:7-9*

God Made Outer Space

written by **HENO HEAD, JR.**
illustrated by **RUSTY FLETCHER**

The Bible's first words are "In the beginning God created the heavens and earth." All was dark and empty, lonely and quiet before creation.

Create means "to make." When God created, he made things. He made lots of things to fill the place we call OUTER SPACE. He scattered stars across space, sparkling up the darkness.

God didn't make all stars the same size. That would be too boring. Instead, he made some stars HUGE. Others are medium-sized. And some are small.

In church or school, you may get stars for doing good work. Those stars usually look like this.

But God made his stars round. Keep reading and you'll find out why.

God made the stars in so many colors—red, orange, yellow, white, blue.

The colors come from the heat of the stars, because all of the stars are hot!

The red and orange stars are hot. Yellow and white stars are even hotter. And the blue stars? Don't even ask. Blue stars are the hottest of them all!

God put all the stars into big groups. We call these giant groups of stars GALAXIES. Some galaxies are shaped like footballs. Others look like pinwheels. God made galaxies in any shape he wanted.

God made all of the galaxies throughout the universe. Just one galaxy has more stars in it than you could count in your whole lifetime. Didn't God make lots of stars?

The MILKY WAY is the name of our galaxy. The stars we see at night are part of that galaxy. Milky Way stars are sprinkled across our nighttime sky just like sugar on blackberries.

As we look at the stars at night, we can see patterns in the sky. These patterns are called CONSTELLATIONS.

There is even a constellation that looks like a man hunting. It's called Orion, the Hunter.

Of all the stars God made, there is one we really like. It's the closest star to us, and it's called the SUN.

Compared to other stars, the Sun is just medium-sized. It's hot, yellow, round, and bright.

The Sun is made of hot gases that produce lots of energy. We see the Sun's energy as sunlight, and we feel it as heat.

Earth seems like a pretty big place to us, but the Sun is much, much bigger than Earth. Over a hundred Earths could fit side by side across the middle of the Sun.

If the Sun were hollow, it would take a million Earths to fill it up.

God put Earth at just the right distance from the Sun. Not too close, or we would get too hot. *Whew!* Not too far, or we would be too cold. *Brrrr!* But just right.

Earth is called a PLANET. A planet is a ball of rock or gas, or both, that travels around a star. We are in a family with eight other planets. The nine planets, plus the Sun, make up what we call the SOLAR SYSTEM.

Each planet is so pretty—and so different from each other.

Little Mercury has craters all over it but no air around it. Venus, often called the Evening Star, has thick clouds and very high heat.

Earth is beautiful—blue and green. Mars, the red planet, has mountains and dry riverbeds.

Giant Jupiter has bands of clouds and a constant storm called the Great Red Spot. As the largest planet, Jupiter is over a thousand times bigger than Earth.

Saturn is the planet with the most beautiful rings.

Distant Uranus, Neptune, and Pluto are icy cold planets.

Jupiter, Saturn, Uranus, and Neptune are the largest planets. Each is made of gas. These four planets have rings around them.

Along with the planets, God made the MOONS. Moons are smaller bodies that travel around planets. The moons shine by reflecting light from the Sun.

Earth has one moon. Mars has two moons. Saturn has 20 moons! Poor Mercury and Venus have no moons at all.

God also created COMETS. Comets are made of ice and rock. Sometimes they are called "dirty snowballs."

He made ASTEROIDS too. Asteroids are large rocks found between Mars and Jupiter.

And God made METEORS. Meteors are tiny rock fragments from comets. God was busy!

God was almost finished creating the universe. With his words, he stirred up space and everything began to spin. The great pinwheel galaxies began to slowly spiral around. All the stars started rotating.

Remember how I told you God made the stars round? Round is the perfect shape for spinning!

The planets have two motions. They spin around like tops and they also travel around the Sun.

Moons move around the planets. Comets and asteroids start their silent journeys around the Sun.

The meteors drift through space. Sometimes they enter Earth's air, speeding up and heating up. They leave quick trails across the night sky—streaks called shooting stars.

God made outer space such an exciting place! When he had finished creating the planets and moons and stars, God looked at all that he had made. And he said, "It is good."

You can read more about God's creation in the Bible! Just look up Genesis, Chapter 1.

BUSY
FEET

written by ELAINE WATSON
illustrated by ROBERTA K. LOMAN

God planned for feet.
Feet are what you stand on. Each foot has five toes. You
have one foot at the end of each leg. When you
stand on your toes, you are taller.
Feet go with you everywhere. Feet are very busy.
Your feet go first when you get out of bed in the morning.
Feet walk you to the kitchen to eat breakfast.
Feet walk you to a friend's house. They walk you into
a church.

But feet can do more than walk. Feet run! They run with your dog. They run to meet Mommy and Daddy coming home.

Feet climb up and down. Feet hop and jump. Feet kick. Feet pedal.

Feet wear shoes and socks (most of the time). Feet wear slippers when you get ready for bed. In the summer feet wear sandals.

When you go swimming and when you take a bath, feet don't wear anything.

Feet are ticklish. At night your feet are the last part of you to get into bed.

Thank you, God, for feet that walk, run, climb, hop, jump, kick, and pedal.

Thank you for my busy feet!

He makes my feet like the feet of a deer. —Psalm 18:33

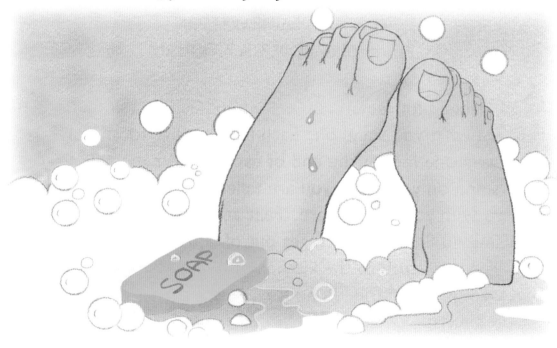

HOW GOD GIVES US POPCORN

written by HENRIETTA D. GAMBILL

illustrated by KATHRYN HUTTON

God gives us crunchy, munchy popcorn to eat and enjoy.

Like magic, it pops! *Pops!* *POPS!* into a fluffy cloud of whiteness.

People have enjoyed eating this fun food for a long, long time.

American Indians were eating popcorn long before Christopher Columbus came to the New World. The Indians popped their popcorn in clay pots filled with very hot sand. The hot sand made the popcorn pop.

Columbus was surprised when he saw the Indians wearing necklaces and other jewelry made of popcorn!

An Indian brought popcorn to the first Thanksgiving feast as a gift to the Pilgrims. He carried it in a big deerskin bag. The Indian's name was Quadequina. He was the brother of the great Indian chief, Massasoit.

But popcorn is much older than the time of the American Indians and the Pilgrims.

Some tiny ears of popcorn were found in a cave in New Mexico by explorers. They think those ears were over 5,000 years old!

Today, Americans eat millions of pounds of popcorn each year.

Most of our popcorn is grown in just four states: Indiana, Ohio, Nebraska, and Iowa. Those states are in the great Corn Belt in the middle of the United States.

Popcorn is planted in the springtime in God's rich, moist soil. Then God's warm sunshine, gentle raindrops, and soft breezes make the popcorn grow.

It grows for about six months, until the kernels have just the right amount of moisture in them. Then sometime in October, the popcorn is harvested.

The moisture or wetness inside the kernels is what makes popcorn pop.

When popcorn is heated, the moisture inside the kernels turns to steam. The steam in the kernels gets hotter and hotter until . . . suddenly . . . *pop! Pop! POP!*

The kernels "explode" and turn inside out! Then we have the crunchy, munchy, white goodness we love to eat. **Popcorn!**

God Made Puppies

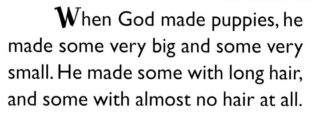

written by MARIAN BENNETT
illustrated by MICHELLE LASH-RUFF

When God made puppies, he made some very big and some very small. He made some with long hair, and some with almost no hair at all.

God gave some pups a long tail, and others just a puff. While some pups may be round and roly-poly, others are light as fluff.

Sometimes puppies can be very good, and sometimes they are very bad! Some pups make us laugh, while others look so sad.

A puppy has a wagging tail and a cool, wet nose, a little pink tongue, and lots of toes!

Puppies like to bite and chew. They may even like to chew on you!

Puppies need good food to eat, water to drink and plenty of rest.

Puppies like all kinds of people—moms and dads, grandpas and grandmas, and YOU the best!

God Made Dinosaurs

written by HENO HEAD, JR.
illustrated by RUSTY FLETCHER

Genesis 1 tells us that God made all of the animals on the earth. He made tiny fuzzy ones and creepy crawly ones, big wrinkly ones and sleek snarly ones—all sizes, shapes, and colors! But some of the most amazing animals God made were . . . the DINOSAURS!

The word *dinosaur* means "terrible lizard." Dinosaurs and lizards are kinds of REPTILES—animals that have scaly skin, breathe with lungs, and usually lay eggs. Maybe you don't think dinosaurs are terrible now, but what if you had one for a neighbor?

Of course that couldn't happen because dinosaurs are EXTINCT. No more dinosaurs are living on the earth. So what do scientists use to find out about dinosaurs?

If you said FOSSILS, you are right! Fossils are rocks that contain old parts or prints of an animal or plant that died some time ago. Scientists use fossils to figure out what the lives of the dinosaurs were like. Some people who study ancient life are called PALEONTOLOGISTS (PAY-lee-on-TOL-uh-jists).

That is a big name, but digging up dinosaur fossils is a big job! First the workers make a map of where the digging will be done. Then they take pictures of the area. Next they measure the found objects, such as dinosaur bones! Finally, the bones are chipped out of the rock, bit by bit.

Paleontologists bring these fossil bones to a MUSEUM. The museum workers make plastic bones that look just like the fossil ones. They put these plastic bones together with metal rods to form a dinosaur skeleton.

We know that reptiles have SCALY skin, but this skin can be any kind of color! Some scientists think some dinosaurs had green and brown skin to blend in with their environment and help them hide from the scary meat-eating dinosaurs.

But dinosaurs may have had brightly colored skin in red or yellow or blue or even with beautiful patterns! God is such an amazing designer—he can do anything!

Dinosaurs came in all sizes. One of the smallest was tiny COMPSOGNATHUS (COMP-sug-NAY-thus). No taller than a chicken, this little dinosaur had to make sure it didn't get under the feet of a slow-moving, long-necked DIPLODOCUS (dih-PLOD-oh-kus).

Other dinosaurs were huge. BRACHIOSAURUS (BRACK-ee-oh-SAWR-us) was as tall as a five-story building and weighed as much as seven school buses!

Dinosaurs ate all kinds of things. ALLOSAURUS (AL-oh-SAWR-us) had very sharp teeth. Running on two strong back legs, a hungry allosaurus chased other dinosaurs, trying to catch them for its dinner!

Sometimes the allosaurus stalked STEGOSAURUS (STEG-oh- SAWR-us), a plant-eating dinosaur that walked on four legs. God gave the stegosaurus hard, upright plates along its back and four sharp spikes on its tail for protection.

Another plant-eater was the TRICERATOPS (try-SAIR-uh-tops). Its name means "three-horned face." Triceratops also had a hard beak for digging up plant roots. The shield behind its huge head gave the triceratops protection from the TYRANNOSAURUS REX (ty-RAN-uh-SAWR-us REX).

This dinosaur's name means "king of the tyrant lizards." The tyrannosaurus, or T. Rex, had a huge jaw with 50 to 60 big, sharp teeth—its teeth were around six inches long! About 40 feet long from head to tail, the tyrannosaurus was one of the most feared dinosaurs.

Smaller but just as fierce was the VELOCIRAPTOR (vuh-LAH-suh-RAP-ter). Its name means "speedy thief." This fast reptile had very sharp claws on its feet. Velociraptors attacked even large animals like the P R O T O C E R A T O P S (PROH-tuh-SAIR-uh-tops)—30 times heavier than the velociraptor!

Protoceratops may have lived in herds. People have found large groups of their nests together. Their nests usually contained 12 or more eggs, laid in a spiral shape.

Many new fossils are discovered every year. Recently, fossils of the largest known meat-eating dinosaur were found in South America. This dinosaur, GIGANOTOSAURUS (jy-GAN-uh-toe-SAWR-us), was even bigger than T. Rex. A car could fit between the huge back legs of the giganotosaurus!

No one knows for sure why all of the dinosaurs died. But because of the fossils that have been found, we can know that these amazing creatures lived! We can also know that God made them! Thank you, God, for creating all life on earth!

BILLIONS OF BUGS

June Bug   Luna Moth   Honeybee

Black & Yellow Argiope   House Mosquito   Nine-Spot Ladybug

written by CLARE MISHICA

illustrated by ROBERTA K. LOMAN

God made **BILLIONS of bugs!** Bugs live in the icy arctic, in hot, sandy deserts, and even inside deep, dark caves.

Thousands of bugs live right in your own yard. Busy ants are crawling back and forth. A spider is weaving a web on your swing set. A butterfly flutters over a patch of red clover.

There's a bug called a walkingstick that hides in trees.

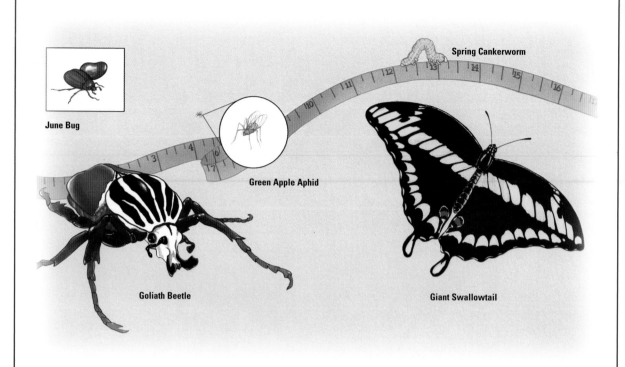

June Bug

Spring Cankerworm

Green Apple Aphid

Goliath Beetle

Giant Swallowtail

He looks like a tiny twig with legs.

A daddy longlegs tiptoes up the steps of your back porch.

What other bugs can you find in your yard?

Bugs come in different sizes. The june bug is as big as a jellybean. The aphid is as tiny as a freckle on your face.

One type of beetle is called Goliath because of his size—4 inches long.

A little caterpillar is called an inchworm. Can you guess why? A giant swallowtail butterfly can have wings as wide as this page!

Bugs come in different colors too. The luna moth is light green. Some beetles look like they are made of yellow gold. The ladybug is round and red.

Some treehoppers are green and scarlet. The gypsy moth caterpillar has red and blue spots.

God gave some bugs special colors to help them hide. The praying mantis is green and brown like a branch.

The katydid has green wings that look like leaves. What do the colors of the moth's wings look like? *Tree bark.*

Some bugs glow. Dancing fireflies flash in the night. Firefly babies glow in the dark. Can you guess their name? *Glowworms!*

The brightest bug is a big click beetle. He looks like a little car with two greenish lights in front and a red one in the back.

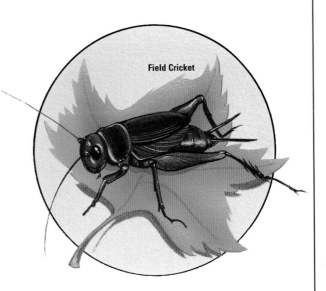

Field Cricket

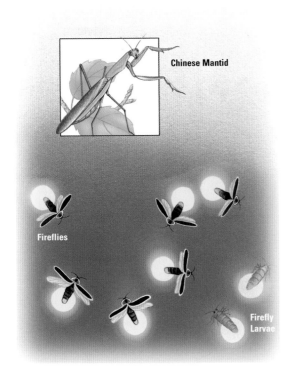

Chinese Mantid

Fireflies

Firefly Larvae

Bugs can be noisy. The click beetle flips over with a *C-L-I-C-K!* Grasshopper wings go *W-H-I-R-R-R-R-R-R!* Busy bumblebees *B-U-Z-Z-Z-Z-Z-Z* from flower top to flower top.

Crickets make music with their wings. Pesky mosquitoes *H-U-M-M-M-M* around your ears. Swish them away!

But the large woolly bear caterpillar creeps along quietly as he eats his leafy lunch. He doesn't make a peep.

Most bugs have six legs. But the centipede has 30 feet! He wiggles when he walks.

Doodlebugs walk backward into their sand tunnels.

Houseflies can walk upside down. They have sticky pads on their feet. How many legs does a wolf spider have? *Eight.*

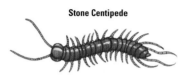

Stone Centipede

Ant Lion Larva

Housefly

Lots of bugs can fly. Dragonflies swoop and soar and dive with their shimmering wings. They even fly backward!

The tiger beetle hides his wings under two shells called sheaths. But come too close and away he goes.

The hover fly zips away from you. Then he zooms right back again.

Some bugs creep and crawl. The earthworm wiggles and wriggles underground. But at night, he comes out to find his dinner. Then back into his tunnel he creeps.

When the millipede is frightened, he curls into a circle and stays very still. Watch him quietly. When he feels safe again, he uncurls and crawls away.

Some bugs even swim. The whirligig twirls and whirls around on the water. The water strider has legs with hairy puffs that keep him afloat. The water beetle dives and darts under the water.

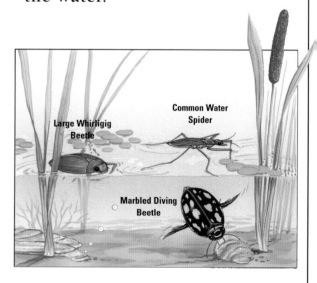

Large Whirligig Beetle

Common Water Spider

Marbled Diving Beetle

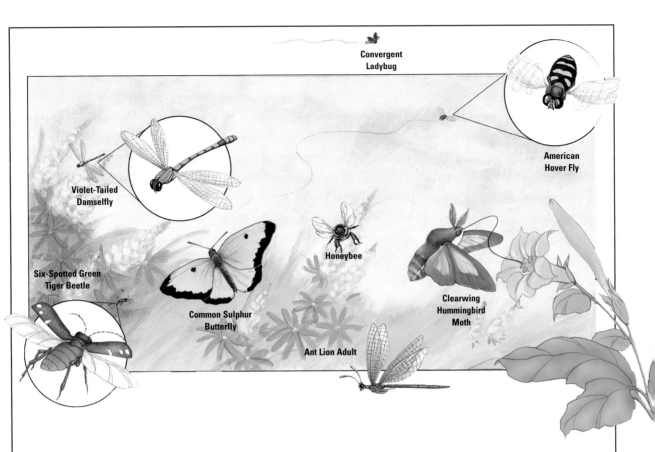

Convergent Ladybug

American Hover Fly

Violet-Tailed Damselfly

Six-Spotted Green Tiger Beetle

Honeybee

Clearwing Hummingbird Moth

Common Sulphur Butterfly

Ant Lion Adult

Some baby spiders climb to the tip of a twig and spin long lines of silk into the wind. Then up, up, up into the sky they float.

Bugs are busy. Fuzzy honeybees spend their summer sipping flower nectar. Other bees are busy too. They make little wax cups with six sides inside the beehive where they live. Nectar put inside the cups turns into a sweet treat—honey!

Before the cold winter comes, the caterpillar is ready. He's safely sleeping inside his chrysalis. When spring arrives he'll be surprised, because he'll be a butterfly!

Papermaking wasps chew up bites of wood and use the pulp to make a paper nest for their babies.

Who comes to your picnic without being asked? Ants! They're looking for food to take home to their anthill. All the ants have jobs to do. Some build and clean. Some take care of the eggs and babies. Only one ant is the queen.

It's best to only watch some bugs—like bees and wasps. They might sting.

But other bugs are safe to hold in your hand. Let a ladybug climb to the top of your finger. She tickles!

A grasshopper sits on your palm for a while. Then—hop, hop, hop—he's gone again! A friendly butterfly may even land on you one day!

Thank you, God, for making BILLIONS of bugs!

How many are your works, O LORD! In wisdom you made them all; the earth is full of your creatures. —*Psalm 104:24*

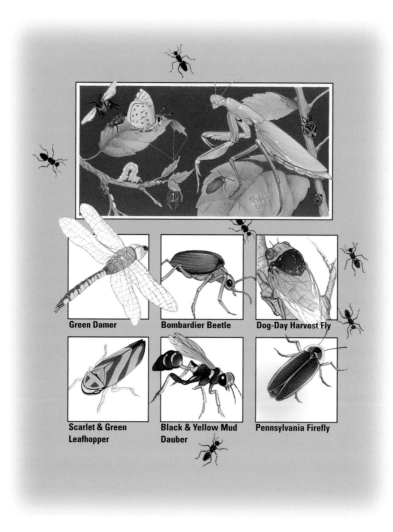

Green Damer

Bombardier Beetle

Dog-Day Harvest Fly

Scarlet & Green Leafhopper

Black & Yellow Mud Dauber

Pennsylvania Firefly

God Made the Ocean

written by HENO HEAD, JR.
illustrated by RUSTY FLETCHER

In the first chapter of the Bible, we can read about the creation of our planet. God said that the water under the sky should all be gathered together to let the dry land appear. God called the water SEAS. And God saw that this was good.

Why are the seas so good? Well, let's find out!

If we look at a globe or a map of the earth, we can see that the seas on the earth are all connected. There's really just one big sea or OCEAN. The ocean takes up about 70 percent of the space on the surface of the earth.

God gave us a lot of water, didn't he? He knew that we would need water to do many, many things. We need water to keep ourselves clean, to make plants grow, to wash our clothes, and of course, to drink! But would you want to take a drink of ocean water?

No way! Ocean water is filled with SALT. And salty water tastes yucky! Where does all this salt come from? Does God have a giant saltshaker in heaven? No!

A lot of salt comes from the land. Water runs down mountains and hills in streams and creeks and rivers. This water picks up tiny bits of salt from the rocks over which it flows. The rivers carry the salt to the ocean.

Some salt also comes from underwater volcanoes. Yes, there are volcanoes under the ocean!

The bottom of the ocean, or the OCEAN FLOOR, is shaped much like the surface of the land—there are mountains, ridges, plains, canyons, valleys, and volcanoes.

Some of the volcanoes are so big that we see the tops of them as ISLANDS, pieces of land totally surrounded by water. The islands of Hawaii are actually the tops of underwater volcanoes!

The ocean floor also has some very deep valleys and trenches. One spot in the ocean, the Mariana Trench, is sooooo deep that you could put Mt. Everest, the tallest mountain in the world, in that trench. There would still be one and a half miles of water covering the mountain!

Light cannot reach these parts of the ocean. The animals that live down this deep are made in a special way so they can survive the cold, the dark, and the pressure of tons of water. Some even have their own lights!

We'll be sure to find some sun on a beautiful sandy BEACH, a place where the land meets the sea. Have you ever wondered where so much sand comes from?

Just like salt, some sand comes from the land. Rivers carry tiny, tiny chips of rock to the ocean. Other sand grains are made by the pounding of ocean WAVES against the rocks along the coast. Millions of these little rock chips get washed up onto the land by the waves, or deposited by the rivers, forming sandy beaches.

Waves roll into the beaches all day long. Do you know what causes waves? If you said WIND, you are right. Wind, or moving air, pushes the ocean water, making waves. Without wind and waves, there couldn't be any surfing or sailboating. Yeah for the wind and the waves!

The ocean is never boring. Twice each day the ocean level rises, and twice each day the ocean level falls. These daily ups and downs of the ocean are called TIDES. The tides are caused mainly by the pull of the gravity of the moon on the ocean water.

low tide

high tide

The moon pulls on the water and the sun heats up the water. Most of the sun's heat strikes the middle of the earth. This area is called the EQUATOR. Water is very warm there. It's in these warm waters that the earth's most powerful storms begin. These huge, swirling storms are called HURRICANES.

Some of the coldest waters are found at the top and bottom of the earth, the POLES. Because there is less direct sunlight there, the ocean freezes and turns into solid ICE. At times big chunks of ice break off and float into the ocean. These floating blocks are called ICEBERGS.

It is so cold at the poles that not many animals can survive there. You may have seen polar bears and penguins at the zoo—but in nature, they are really a world apart! Polar bears live at the North Pole and penguins live mainly at the South Pole.

The ocean water, the sea floor, the sandy beaches, the waves, the tides, the hurricanes, and the icebergs are all special. But do you know what is really amazing in the great ocean God made? The LIFE!

The largest animals in the world, WHALES, are found in the ocean. The biggest whale is the blue whale. It is long enough for six elephants to ride on its back.

Whales are not FISH; they are MAMMALS. Fish breathe with gills. Mammals breathe with lungs. That is why whales have to come up for air. Dolphins also are mammals.

God filled the ocean with all kinds of fish—big fish, little fish, colorful tropical fish, and funny-faced fish. He made fish that look like horses and fish that look like lions. He made flying fish and kissing fish. He even made the starfish and the jellyfish, which aren't really fish at all!

Fish are designed to swim. They have fins and a tail for moving through the water. Most fish also have a SWIM BLADDER, a bag of air that helps them float. But sharks don't have these bladders. Instead, sharks have to swim all the time—even in their sleep! That way they can keep water moving over their GILLS. Fish use gills to breathe.

Sharks and other big ocean creatures such as killer whales, giant squid, and enormous eels may seem pretty scary. And you probably wouldn't want to go swimming with them. But even though they can be dangerous, they are not monsters. They are just more of the amazing kinds of life that God created.

God could have made just one kind of ocean animal. He could have made just one kind of fish, or one kind of crab, or one kind of whale. But he didn't! He made thousands of kinds of animals for us to enjoy, just because he loves us!

So next time you walk along the sandy beach, think about the amazing ocean God made. When God saw that the seas were good, he was right.

And when we say God is good, we are right too!

Bible Stories

"Thank You" taken from

JESUS
Makes Me Happy

written by WANDA HAYES
illustrated by FRANCES HOOK

Wherever Jesus went people said, "Please make me well." Jesus did. He made blind people see. He made lame people walk. He made dead people live. The people knew God's Son could do these things.

One day as Jesus and his friends started to go into a city, they heard some men call, "Jesus, teacher, help us." Jesus saw 10 men who were very sick. They had bad sores on their bodies.

Jesus told them, "Go show yourselves to the priests." The men did what Jesus said. As they were going, they looked at their bodies. The sores were all gone. Jesus had made all 10 men well. How happy they were!

Nine of the men hurried into the city, but one man came running back to Jesus. He knelt at Jesus' feet and said, "Thank you, Jesus. Thank you for making me well."

Jesus was sorry that the other men didn't say thank you. He was very glad that one man did. Jesus knew this man really loved him.

Hurry Up, Noah

written by PATRICIA SHELY MAHANY
illustrated by TERRY JULIEN

God looked down from Heaven. "Look at my people," he said sadly. "They have forgotten all about me. They are very bad."

But there was one man on the earth who was very good. His name was Noah. Noah loved God very much. Noah made God happy.

Hurry up, Noah, and listen to God!

One day God said to Noah, "I want you to make a big, big boat. I will tell you just how to do it."

So God told Noah just how big to make the boat. "Be sure to put a big door in the side of it," he said.

Then God said, "Noah, I want you to take with you two of every kind of animal and bird on the earth." Noah made sure there was plenty of food for all of the animals and his family too.

Hurry up, Noah, and fill the boat!

How busy Noah must have been! But soon he was finished. Then into the big boat went the sneaking snails and tiptoeing turtles. Two by two came the lumbering lions and prancing ponies. Marching monkeys and walking wolves filled the boat. Just

Hurry up, Noah, and build the boat!

Noah got busy right away. He made the boat just the right size. He built the boat just like God told him to do.

Hurry up, Noah, and obey God's Word!

like God said. Then Noah and his family went into the big boat. God closed the door.

Rain! **Rain! RAIN!** For 40 days and 40 nights, rain fell from the sky. Soon water covered the earth. But Noah and his family were safe and dry in the boat.

Hurry up, Noah, and see the rain!

Up! **Up! UP** went the boat, floating on the water. For many days the boat floated on the water. Noah and his family were busy inside the boat taking good care of the animals.

Hurry up, Noah, and feed the elephants!

Woooo! **Woooo! WOOOO!** Do you hear the wind? God sent a big wind to dry up the water.

Hurry up, Noah, and listen to the wind!

Down! **Down! DOWN** went the boat as the water slowly dried up.

One day Noah sent a dove out. He wanted to see if the dove could find dry land. But the land was still covered with water, so the dove flew back into the boat.

Seven days later, Noah sent the dove out again. This time the

dove brought back a brand-new olive leaf. Seven days later Noah sent the dove out again. The dove flew away and did not come back. Then Noah knew that the dove had found a dry place to land.

Hurry up, Noah, and see the dry land!

Soon the earth was completely dry again.

"Noah," God said, "it is time for you to leave the boat."

Hurry up, Noah, and leave the boat!

Out of the boat went leaping leopards and slithering snakes. Skipping skunks and jumping jackrabbits left the big boat. Dancing deer and racing raccoons followed. All of the animals and Noah's family were glad to be out on God's clean earth.

Hurry up, Noah, it's time to thank God!

Noah and his family built an altar to God. "Thank you, God," they said, "for keeping us safe."

God was pleased with his new earth, and he made a promise to Noah.

"Never again will I send a big flood to cover the earth," he said.

And to show his promise, God made a big, beautiful rainbow and put it in the sky.

Hurry up, Noah, and see God's rainbow!

Noah was glad he had obeyed God.

Daniel and the Lions

written and illustrated by HEIDI PETACH

Darius the Mede was king over all the land.

He chose 120 princes to rule under him. Then he chose three presidents to rule the princes.

Daniel was one of the presidents. King Darius liked Daniel the best because he was honest and did what was right.

All the other rulers were jealous of Daniel.

They decided to catch him in a mistake. But no one could find anything wrong. Daniel always worked hard, and he always did a good job.

"There is only one way we can get Daniel," one of the princes said. "Listen! I have a plan. . . ."

Daniel's enemies went to see King Darius. "O king," they said, "we think you should make a law that says for 30 days no one may pray to any god or man except you. Anyone who breaks this law will be thrown into the lions' den. Sign here, Sire."

After Darius signed the law, Daniel's enemies said, "Now it is a law of the Medes and Persians. It can never be changed!"

On top of Daniel's house was a quiet room. He liked praying to God there.

Daniel knew about the new law. But God came first. Three times every day Daniel knelt and prayed to God.

"Aha!" cried Daniel's enemies. They had been watching Daniel. They ran to the king. "Daniel has broken your new law!" they said. "He must be thrown to the lions!"

The king was very upset. He liked Daniel. He tried all day to find a way to change the law.

At the end of the day, Daniel's enemies came back. "You know, O king, that the law of the Medes and Persians can never be changed."

King Darius had to call for Daniel. "May your God, whom you serve so well, save you," he said.

The lions were roaring for their dinner. Soldiers threw Daniel down into the dark den. They put a big stone over the door and poured hot wax around it. The king pressed his signet ring in the wax so that no one would open the door.

King Darius felt terrible. He didn't want any dinner or music. He worried about Daniel all night.

Finally, the sun came up. The king ran to the lions' den. *Was Daniel still alive?* "Daniel!" he called, "has your God saved you?"

"God sent his angel to shut the lions' mouths. Look! I am not even scratched!"

The king was very happy. So were the lions. The men who were Daniel's enemies were tossed into the lions' den and the lions ate them for breakfast.

Then King Darius made a new law. It said, "Everyone must worship Daniel's God, for he is the living God. He saved Daniel from being killed in the lions' den."

The Little Lost Sheep

written by MARILYN LEE LINDSEY
illustrated by RUTH A. O'CONNELL

Once there was a baby sheep who lived with his warm, woolly mother. They lived on a hill with lots of other warm, woolly sheep.

One spring morning the baby sheep decided to take a walk. He wanted to take a walk to see the world that God had made.

The baby sheep walked down the other side of the hill. He looked on the ground. He saw a tiny crocus poking through the soft dirt.

And he was glad.

The baby sheep looked between two rocks. He saw a big, green woolly worm peeking out of the crack.

And he was glad.

The baby sheep walked around a prickly bush that had lots of big thorns on it. He walked on down a rocky hillside. He stopped. He looked back up the hill. Where was his grassy, hill home? Where was his warm, woolly mother?

Then the baby sheep saw a sparrow sitting on a twig of the prickly bush. He asked the tiny bird, "Can you help me find my way home? I want my grassy, hill home. I need my warm, woolly mother."

The sparrow said to the baby sheep, "Don't worry, the good shepherd will find you and take you safely home."

Walking on, the baby sheep saw a lily growing among the grass. He asked the tall, slender flower,

"Can you help me find my way home? I want my grassy, hill home. I need my warm, woolly mother."

The lily said to the baby sheep, "Don't worry, the good shepherd will find you and take you safely home."

As he walked on, the baby sheep saw a badger climbing over some rocks. He asked the small, furry animal, "Can you help me find my way home? I want my grassy, hill home. I need my warm, woolly mother."

The badger said to the baby sheep, "Don't worry, the good shepherd will find you and take you safely home."

But the baby sheep was now so tired, he lay down against a rock and began to cry. He was all alone and afraid. Who could take him safely home?

Then the baby sheep heard something. He stopped crying and lifted his head. Someone was calling to him.

"Come to me, little one," said the good shepherd. "I will take you safely home again."

The baby sheep ran to the shepherd. And the good shepherd gently lifted the baby sheep into his strong arms. He carried the baby sheep to his grassy, hill home. He was safely home again with his warm, woolly mother.

And he was glad.

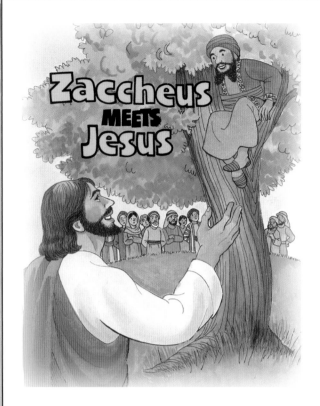

Zaccheus MEETS Jesus

written by DIANE M. STORTZ
illustrated by VERA GOHMAN

Zaccheus, the tax collector, was a rich man, a short man, and a curious man who wanted to see Jesus.

Zaccheus was not a good man. He cheated people. Zaccheus made the people pay more taxes than they really had to pay. Then Zaccheus kept part of the money for himself.

Zaccheus didn't have many friends. The people in the town of Jericho where Zaccheus lived didn't like being cheated.

Zaccheus had heard the people talking about Jesus—how he made sick people well and taught about God's great love. Zaccheus wondered if these things were true.

One day Zaccheus heard a shout, "Jesus is coming!" Men and women and boys and girls ran to the road and lined up to see Jesus as he passed by.

Zaccheus ran too. But he was so short he couldn't find a place to stand. He couldn't see over the heads of the people in the crowd. And no one would let him through to the front of the line.

But Zaccheus didn't give up. He ran to a tree by the side of the road and quickly climbed up into its branches.

He climbed from branch to branch until he could see Jesus walking up the road.

As Jesus came closer to the tree, Zaccheus looked down and saw Jesus looking up at him!

"Zaccheus, hurry and come down," said Jesus. "Today I must stay at your house."

At my house? thought Zaccheus. *No one has ever wanted to come to my house.* Zaccheus hurried down and took Jesus home for dinner.

"Look at that!" complained the people of Jericho. "Jesus has gone to eat with Zaccheus. Everyone knows about the bad things Zaccheus has done."

But at the house of Zaccheus, there was not any complaining. Zaccheus listened to Jesus. He knew the things that Jesus taught were true. Zaccheus was sorry for all the wrong things he had done. He decided to start doing right instead.

Zaccheus stood and said to Jesus, "Lord, half of all I own I will give to the poor. If I have cheated anyone, I will pay him back four times as much."

Jesus was pleased. He said to Zaccheus, "I have come to save everyone who has done wrong."

Now Zaccheus was a rich man, a short man, and a happy man because he decided to do what was right.

Breakfast with Jesus
A STORY FOR EASTER

written by MARK A. TAYLOR
illustrated by ANDY STILES

"I'm cold," said Thomas as the night breeze blew across his wet arms.

"Me too," said Nathanael, and he shivered in the creaky boat.

"I'm hungry," said James as he watched the water and their empty fishing net.

"Me too," said John, and his stomach growled and rumbled.

All the fisherman laughed— all except Peter.

"Keep fishing!" he commanded. It's almost morning, and we haven't caught a thing," Peter sighed.

I wish Jesus were here, he said to himself. *I hope we'll see him again soon.*

Just then the fishermen heard a voice from far away.

"Friends!" said the voice.

"Who's that?" asked Thomas.

"Do you have any fish?"

"The voice is coming from the shore!" said John.

The fishermen didn't know what to think. They didn't know what to say. They peered through the fog and saw a man on the land.

"Do you have any fish?" the man called again.

"No," said Thomas, Nathanael, James, and John.

"No," said Peter.

"No," said all the cold and hungry fishermen in the creaky boat on the quiet lake.

And then the man said something quite surprising. . . . "Throw your net on the other side of the boat."

Thomas looked at Nathanael. James looked at John. They all looked at Peter. And Peter said, "OK, let's try it."

The fishermen tugged the heavy net out of the water and into the boat. Not one fish was in the net. Then they heaved the net back into the water on the other side of the boat.

"There," said Thomas. "We did what he said. But what difference does it make? We'll never catch any fish tonight."

And then it happened! Fish!

The net was full of fish! Swimming, flipping, flopping fish!

The net bulged and almost broke. The men could not haul it back into the boat.

John stared across the water at the man still watching from the shore. "It's Jesus," he said. "It's Jesus! Jesus is the one who told us where to fish!"

"I want to see him!" said Peter. Peter dove into the lake.

Plop, ker-plop!

Jesus told us he would meet us! he remembered as he swam.

Left arm, right arm!

Jesus told us he would live forever!

Kick hard! Hurry, hurry!

Jesus died once but never again!

Peter smiled as he sloshed out of the water onto the sandy shore. There was Jesus, cooking fish over a small fire of hot coals.

Soon the other fishermen brought their net full of fish to shore.

"Come and have breakfast with me," Jesus said.

Jesus gave them bread and fish to eat. "Thank you, God, for

our food," he said. "Thank you for my fishermen friends. Thank you for letting me live again, even after I was dead."

Now Thomas and Nathanael were warm, sitting by the fire Jesus made. And James and John were full, eating the tasty breakfast Jesus cooked.

And Peter—well, Peter sat on the seashore and munched his breakfast and talked with Jesus all morning long.

He couldn't have been happier!

written by HENRIETTA D. GAMBILL

illustrated by JOE BODDY

A long time ago,
There was nothing at all.
No world, sun, or creatures
No people, big or small.

And God didn't like things the way they were.
So God began to think very hard, until he had a plan.
"I'll create the universe," God said,
    "and then I'll make a man."
And God did.

On the first day of creation,
God made daylight so bright,
And darkness, called night.
And God liked the daylight and darkness
   he had made.

On the second day of creation,
God made the big, blue sky
On his very first try!
And God liked the big, blue sky
   he had made.

On the third day of creation,
God made the oceans, lakes, seas,
And the dry land growing trees.
And God liked the oceans, lakes, seas, and trees
   he had made.

On the fourth day of creation,
God made the sun so bright to shine in the day,
And the moon and stars to keep darkness away.
And God liked the sun, moon, and stars
    he had made.

On the fifth day of creation,
God made the big sea creatures, and some very small.
He made birds of every color, who fly but never fall.
And God liked the sea creatures and birds
    he had made.

On the sixth day of creation,
God made all kinds of animals to live on the land,
And then last of all, God made a man.
And God liked the animals and the man
     he had made.

The man God made was Adam.
And Adam was all alone.
"I'll make a woman to help you," God said.
And he did from Adam's rib bone!
And God loved Adam and Eve,
     the first people on earth.

God made a beautiful garden
And gave it to Adam and Eve.
"This garden is yours to live in," God said.
"If you obey, you'll never have to leave."
And God liked the Garden of Eden he had made.

On the seventh day, God said, "I'm done . . .
　　　I've made what I should.
My creation is beautiful.
It's all very good."
Then God rested on the seventh day because
　　　his work of creation was done.

I'm glad that God created
Everything we can see.
But most of all I'm glad
That he loves even me!

Thank you, God.

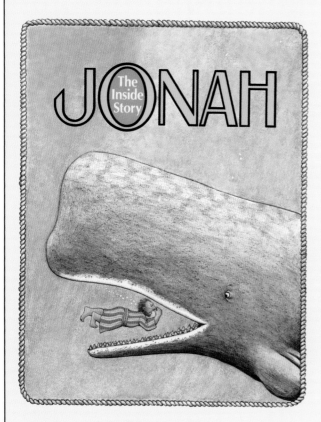

JONAH
The Inside Story

written and illustrated by
HEIDI PETACH

Long, long ago God talked to a man called Jonah.

"Jonah," he said, "I want you to go to the great city of Nineveh. Tell the people there that I am tired of seeing them be so mean."

"What!" cried Jonah, surprised. "I can't go there! The people of Nineveh are bullies. They have been doing bad things to my friends and neighbors for a long time."

Nineveh was the last place on earth Jonah wanted to go.

So instead of obeying God and going to the big city of Nineveh, Jonah left on a ship that was sailing in the opposite direction—all the way across the sea to Tarshish.

But God was watching Jonah. He sent a great wind to blow the sea into huge, rocking waves. *Whoosh!* The ship was tossed about like a tiny toy.

The sailors were afraid the boat would sink because of the heavy load it carried, so they threw the cargo overboard into the sea.

Everyone on the ship was frightened. Everyone except Jonah. Where was he?

Fast asleep, snoring!

"Wake up!" shouted the ship's captain. "How can you sleep at a time like this? Call on your God to save us!"

But Jonah wouldn't. He was trying to run away from God.

Splash! Crash! The storm got worse. The people decided God was punishing someone on the ship. They drew straws to see who it was. The one who pulled the shortest straw would be the guilty one. Guess who pulled it?

"I am the one," Jonah admitted. "God is very angry with me for disobeying him. Throw me overboard and the storm will go away."

But the sailors did not want to throw Jonah overboard. Instead, they rowed hard to try to bring the ship back to land as the wind roared louder and the waves rolled higher.

Finally, the sailors became so afraid that they gave up and threw Jonah overboard into the sea.

Was this the end of Jonah? No. God had a plan to save him.

Deep, deep down in the sea lived a huge, fish-like creature. God had made it especially to take care of Jonah.

With a big gulp, it swallowed Jonah whole so he wouldn't drown.

For three days and three nights, Jonah lived inside the huge animal where it was like a dark, slippery cave.

But Jonah prayed while he was inside the creature. He thanked God that he was alive.

Then God spoke to the big sea creature and told it to spit Jonah out on a beach. It was glad to get rid of Jonah. Jonah gave it a tummy ache!

Finally, Jonah obeyed God and went to the city of Nineveh and preached to the people. Jonah said, "In 40 days God will flatten your city because you have been acting so mean!"

Then the people of Nineveh were sorry they had been so bad. Even the king himself believed in God and promised to be better.

This made God very happy. He was glad he didn't have to destroy the city and could save the people of Nineveh.

But Jonah wasn't happy at all. He had liked feeling better than the people of Nineveh. He didn't want God to forgive them.

Hoping God would change his mind and flatten Nineveh after all, Jonah sat outside the city and waited to see what would happen next.

Soon the sun was high overhead, heating Jonah till he felt like he was sizzling in a frying pan.

To cool off, poor Jonah built a tent-like shelter for shade. Meanwhile, God made a vine to grow up and shade Jonah even more. What a relief! Jonah felt a lot better then.

But the next day, God sent a hungry worm to eat the vine.

This made Jonah angry, and he cried out, "Lord, why did you let that poor plant die?"

Then God told Jonah, "You felt sorry for the plant, but you don't want me to feel sorry for the people of Nineveh. Shouldn't I forgive those who turn to me, no matter who they are?"

Finally, Jonah understood what God had been trying to teach him. He went back home and wrote this story telling us how much God loves *everyone*.

My Story of Jesus

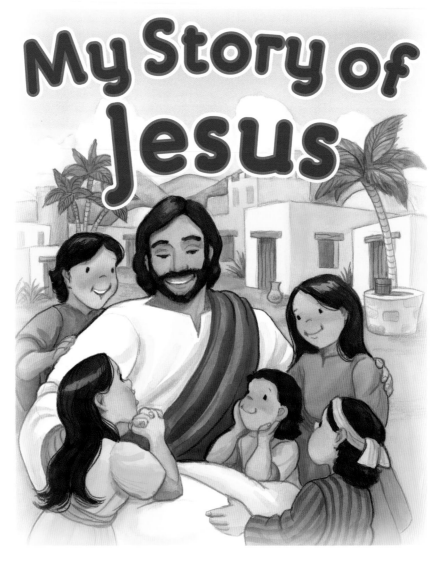

written by JENNIFER HOLDER
illustrated by NANCY MUNGER

Long ago, God said that he would send his Son to be the Savior and king of his people.

God's Son, Jesus, was born in Bethlehem. His mother, Mary, wrapped him in cloths and laid him in a manger.

Some shepherds hurried from the fields to worship the new baby king.

As Jesus grew up, he obeyed his parents and pleased God. When he was 12, Jesus went with his family to God's temple in Jerusalem.

He talked with the priests and teachers about God's teachings and God's love. They were amazed at how much Jesus understood.

A man named John was telling people about Jesus.

"Good news!" he said. "God has sent Jesus to save us. We need to get ready for him!" People came to John to be baptized.

Jesus came to be baptized too. When Jesus came up from the water, God's Spirit came from Heaven like a dove. Then a voice from Heaven said, "You are my Son. I love you. I am pleased with you."

Then Jesus began to do the work God had planned for him.

Jesus showed God's care and concern for people. He made sick people well and made blind people see. He even made lame people able to walk!

Jesus showed God's power. One day when Jesus and some of his followers were in a boat, a terrible storm came up.

The followers were afraid, but Jesus told the wind and waves, "Quiet! Be still!" And the storm stopped.

Jesus was a teacher. He taught people about God's love. He told them to love God and to love each other. Jesus became known as a wonderful teacher.

Mothers and fathers brought their children to Jesus so that he could bless them and pray for them.

Jesus went to Jerusalem for a special celebration that is called Passover. He entered the city on a donkey, and crowds cheered for him. They called him their king and placed palm branches at his feet.

In Jerusalem Jesus ate the Passover meal with his followers. He told them he would leave them soon.

Then Jesus showed his followers a special way to

always remember him. He gave thanks to God, broke bread, and passed it to his followers. He passed his cup to them too. "Remember me when you eat this bread and drink from this cup," said Jesus.

Jesus was ready to finish the work that God had planned for him. That meant he must die. This was part of God's plan for saving people from sin.

buried Jesus' body in a tomb and closed it with a heavy stone.

Jesus died on a wooden cross. His followers were very sad. They

But when some women went back to Jesus' tomb, they were surprised to find the stone was rolled away and the tomb was empty!

Suddenly, they saw an angel. "Jesus is not here," the angel told the women. "He is alive again!"

Many people saw Jesus after he had risen. Jesus told his followers, "Go everywhere and tell everyone the good news about me!"

Jesus returned to Heaven to make a new home for his followers. But he promised to come back again one day. What a happy day that will

Stories About
Faith and Family

Can God See Me?

written by JODEE MCCONNAUGHHAY

illustrated by MAX KOLDING

Matthew looked up at the stars. So many. So far away.

Matthew wondered, *Is God farther than the stars? Can God see me from so far?*

Grandpa was older and smarter than Matthew. Maybe he would know. And besides . . .

Grandpa was right there.

"Grandpa?" said Matthew.

"Yes?" Grandpa answered.

"Is God farther than the stars? I just want to know. Can he see me here—way down below?"

"The Bible tells us 'The Lord watches over all who love him,'"

Grandpa said. "You're never too far for God to see you."

"Inside our dark tent, can God see me? How? Tell me, please, Grandpa. I want to know now."

"'The Lord watches over all who love him,'" Grandpa said. "You can't hide from God—even in the dark."

"But when I'm in a crowd, I feel so small. Can God tell it's me—not Patti or Paul?"

"'The Lord watches over all who love him,'" Grandpa said. "He knows it's you. He knows your name."

"What if I stay in a hospital bed? Will God know I'm there— not home instead?"

"'The Lord watches over all who love him,'" Grandpa said. "God sees each time you hurt or cry, and he knows what you need to get well."

"What if I lived in an igloo of ice? Could God see me there and call my name once or twice?"

"'The Lord watches over all who love him,'" Grandpa said. "That means God sees you wherever you are."

"Even in a submarine deep in the sea? Under the water can God still see me?"

"'The Lord watches over all who love him,'" Grandpa said. "And God made the oceans—so he knows where to find you."

"If I'm in a spaceship waaay past the moon, would I be closer to God than I am in my room?"

"Matthew," Grandpa said, "God is everywhere. He's as close as our hearts. He's as near as a prayer."

Matthew stared at the sky. Then opening his arms as wide as could be, he said, "'The Lord watches over all who love him'—and that means ME!"

The LORD *watches over all who love him.*
—Psalm 145:20

I'm glad I'm your Grandma

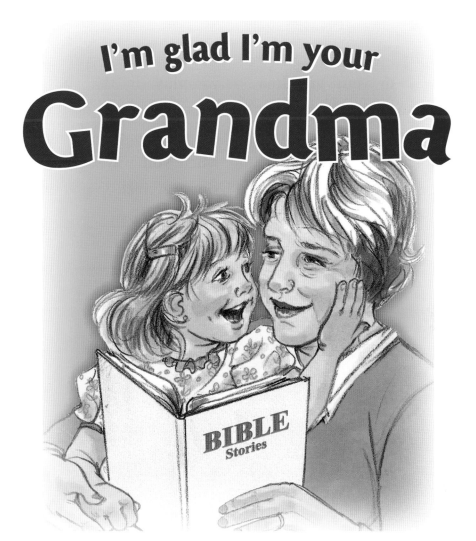

written by BILL AND KATHY HORLACHER
illustrated by MEREDITH JOHNSON

I'm glad I'm your grandma! Please let me say why:

I'm glad I'm your grandma when we go for a walk—or sit on the porch just to have a nice talk.

I'm glad I'm your grandma when you send me a card—or you paint me a picture, which shows you've tried hard.

I'm glad I'm your grandma when you call on the phone—or you come for a visit just to see me at home.

I'm glad I'm your grandma when we share something sweet—

and with a big smile you say, "Thanks for the treat!"

I'm glad I'm your grandma when we ride in the car—or when it's dark and we see a bright star.

I'm glad I'm your grandma when you give a squeeze—or you ask for a favor and politely say "Please."

I'm glad I'm your grandma when we take time to play—and when talking to God you have plenty to say.

I'm glad I'm your grandma when we go to the park—and we play on the swings until it gets dark.

I'm glad I'm your grandma when you wave good night—or I sing you to sleep and then tuck you in tight.

But most of all, I'm glad I'm your grandma . . . just because you're you. You're God's wonderful gift to me!

Sing Praises!

illustrated by KATHY MARLIN

Jesus Loves Me

Jesus loves me, this I know,
For the Bible tells me so;
Little ones to him belong;
They are weak, but he is strong.
Yes, Jesus loves me!
Yes, Jesus loves me!
Yes, Jesus loves me!
The Bible tells me so!

The B-I-B-L-E
The B-I-B-L-E,
Yes, that's the book for me,
I stand alone on the Word of God,
The B-I-B-L-E. Bible!

This Little Light of Mine
This little light of mine,
I'm gonna let it shine.
This little light of mine,
I'm gonna let it shine,
This little light of mine,
I'm gonna let it shine,
Let it shine, let it shine, let it shine.

Rise and Shine

The Lord said to Noah,
There's gonna be a floody, floody.
The Lord said to Noah,
There's gonna be a floody, floody.
Get those animals (clap!)
Out of the muddy, muddy,
Children of the Lord.

So rise and shine,
And give God the glory, glory.
Rise and shine,
And give God the glory, glory.
Rise and shine and (clap!)
Give God the glory, glory,
Children of the Lord!

Jesus Is a Friend

(to the tune of "Ten Little Indians")
Jesus is a friend to little children.
Jesus is a friend to little children.
Jesus is a friend to little children.
I want to be like Jesus.

Jesus Loves the Little Children

Jesus loves the little children,
All the children of the world.
Red and yellow, black and white,
They are precious in his sight.
Jesus loves the little children of the world.

For the Beauty of the Earth

For the beauty of the earth,
For the glory of the skies,
For the love which from our birth
Over and around us lies,
Lord of all, to thee we raise
This our hymn of grateful praise.

For the joy of human love,
Brother, sister, parent, child,
Friends on earth and friends above,
For all gentle thoughts and mild,
Lord of all, to thee we raise
This our hymn of grateful praise.

Go, Tell It on the Mountain

Go, tell it on the mountain,
Over the hills and everywhere!
Go, tell it on the mountain,
That Jesus Christ is Lord!

Will You Tell a Friend?

(to the tune of "Muffin Man")
Will you tell a friend today,
A friend today, a friend today?
Will you tell a friend today
That Jesus is God's Son?

God Is So Good

God is so good,
God is so good,
God is so good,
He's so good to me.

Jesus, Jesus, I Love You

(to the tune of "Twinkle, Twinkle")
Jesus, Jesus, I love you,
Teach me all that I should do.
I will talk to you each day,
Follow you in every way.
Jesus, Jesus, I love you,
I'm so glad you love me too.

He's Got the Whole World

He's got the whole world in His hands,
He's got the whole wide world in His hands,
He's got the whole world in His hands,
He's got the whole world in His hands.

He's got all the little children in His hands,
He's got all the little children in His hands,
He's got all the little children in His hands,
He's got the whole world in His hands.

If You're Happy and You Know It

If you're happy and you know it,
Praise the Lord! (Amen!)
If you're happy and you know it,
Praise the Lord! (Amen!)
If you're happy and you know it,
Then your life will surely show it.
If you're happy and you know it,
Praise the Lord! (Amen!)

Joyful, Joyful, We Adore Thee

Joyful, joyful, we adore thee,
God of glory, Lord of love;
Hearts unfold like flowers before thee,
Opening to the sun above.
Melt the clouds of sin and sadness;
Drive the dark of doubt away;
Giver of immortal gladness,
Fill us with the light of day!

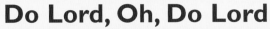

Do Lord, Oh, Do Lord

I've got a home in glory land that outshines the sun.
I've got a home in glory land that outshines the sun.
I've got a home in glory land that outshines the sun,
Away beyond the blue.
Do Lord, oh, do Lord, oh, do remember me.
Do Lord, oh, do Lord, oh, do remember me.
Do Lord, oh, do Lord, oh, do remember me,
Away beyond the blue.

Doxology

Praise God, from whom all blessings flow;
Praise him, all creatures here below;
Praise him above, ye heavenly host;
Praise Father, Son, and Holy Ghost.
Amen.

God Made You Special

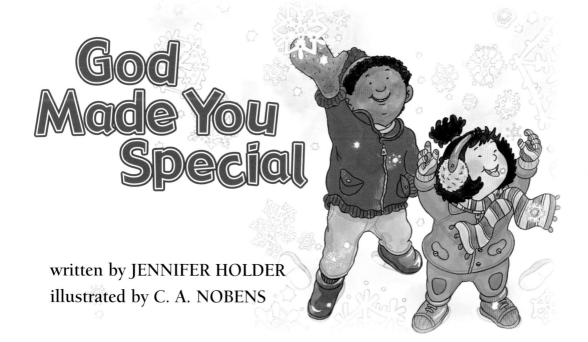

written by JENNIFER HOLDER
illustrated by C. A. NOBENS

God made you special.

Just as no two snowflakes are identical . . . just as no two thumbprints are the same . . . God made each person different. God made each person *special*.

Some people are tall. And some people are short. Some people are dark. And some people are light.

Some people have strong hands. Others have warm smiles. Some people have beautiful eyes. And every person is special.

There are billions of people in the world—but there is only *one* you. That's *special!*

Yes, God made you special.

Can you paint pictures? Can you catch a baseball? Can you sing a song? Whatever you can do well is a talent God gave to you.

And God planned ways for you to use your talents so you can serve him and help others.

You can help someone learn to paint. You can play catch with someone who is lonely. You can sing praise to God. You can do lots of special things.

There is one reason you are special that is more important than any other. You are special because God made you. You are like him. That's why you can *feel . . . think . . . imagine . . .* and *create*. God does those things.

God made everyone in his own image. He loves everyone. God's Son, Jesus, loves everyone too. Jesus wants to be our friend.

Jesus came to earth so that one day you can live with him in Heaven. Being made in God's image is very special.

Yes, God made you. He loves you, and he thinks you're special. So do I. Let's thank God for making you special.

God created human beings in his image.
—Genesis 1:27

What Is Faith?

written by VIRGINIA MUELLER

illustrated by MAX KOLDING

Faith is seeing with your heart what you cannot see with your eyes.

It is planting a seed and patiently waiting for the seed to grow into a flower.

It is finding a caterpillar and believing that someday the caterpillar will change into a butterfly.

Faith is seeing the eggs in a nest and trusting that they will hatch.

Faith is praying to God and knowing that he is listening.

Faith is knowing God has power over everything—even the big nighttime sky.

Sometimes having faith means giving all that you have to someone else . . . because you know God will always give you everything that you need.

Faith is always being God's friend and doing things when they are hard . . . because you trust him.

Faith is looking for God and finding his love in your family . . . and in your friends.

Faith is knowing God is always with you even though you don't see his face.

Whenever you hear a bird's song . . . Whenever you feel a soft, warm kitten . . . Whenever you smell a sweet flower . . . Whenever you see a rainbow after the rain . . . Faith is believing God made all these things because he loves you.

Faith is trusting. Faith is hoping. Faith is believing.

Faith is depending on God to keep all of his promises—and saying thank-you because he always does.

Faith means being sure of the things we hope for. And faith means knowing that something is real even if we do not see it.
—Hebrews 11:1

JESUS LOVES ME
All the time

written by E. ELAINE WATSON
illustrated by LORRAINE ARTHUR

Jesus loves me, this is true,
Wherever I am or whatever I do.

Jesus loves me at lunchtime,
Playtime,
Bedtime,
Anytime,
Every time,
All the time.
That's when Jesus loves me.

When I am climbing up a tree,
Or when I am swimming in the sea,
Jesus loves me.

When I am walking down the street,
Or when I am sitting in my seat,
Jesus loves me.

When I cry for my broken toy,
Or when I am laughing and full of joy,
Jesus loves me.

He loves me at lunchtime,
Breakfast time,
Suppertime,
Anytime,
Every time,
All the time.
That's when Jesus loves me.

When I am riding around on my bike,
Or when Daddy helps me fly my kite,
Jesus loves me.

When I am feeding bread to my duck,
Or when I share my brand-new truck,
Jesus loves me.

Jesus loves me at lunchtime,
Summertime,
Wintertime,
Anytime,
Every time,
All the time.
That's when Jesus loves me.

Jesus loves me, this is true,
Wherever I am or whatever I do.
And I want to love Jesus all the time too.

I'll love him at lunchtime,

Breakfast time,

Suppertime,

Playtime,

Wintertime,

Summertime,

Bedtime,

Anytime,

Every time,

All the time.

That's when I want to love Jesus,
Because that's when Jesus loves me.

I Can Pray!

written by JENNIFER HOLDER AND DIANE STORTZ
illustrated by C. A. NOBENS

I can pray! Praying is talking and listening to God.

I have lots of things to say to God in my prayers.

When I pray, I praise God. He is awesome and powerful. Every day God does wonderful things.

When I pray, I confess. When I ran through Mrs. Nelson's flower beds—even after Mom told me not to—I prayed to God. I told him that I had done something wrong.

After I was mean to my sister, I confessed that to God too.

When I pray, I thank God for his blessings. I tell him I am

grateful for my family, friends, and church.

When I pray, I ask God for his help. If I have a problem, I tell God about it. I ask him to help other people with their problems too. When my friend's dad was sick, I asked God to help him get better, and he did!

"Give all your worries to him." 1 Peter 5:7

God wants me to talk to him, but he also wants to talk to me, so I listen to God.

I *listen* to God when I read the Bible. The Bible is God's Word.

God guides me and gives me wisdom. He helps me know what is right.

Sometimes when I want to talk, my friends are too busy. And sometimes nobody is home. But God is never too busy for me to talk to him. I can talk to God anytime.

When I'm in the car . . . or walking my dog . . . or doing my chores . . . I can pray to God!

Sometimes my family takes trips to places far, far away. That's OK because I can still talk to God!

Whether I'm at home . . . or at

school . . . even if I were swimming deep in the ocean . . . or floating through outer space . . . God is still near me, listening to my prayers. Isn't God amazing?

There are lots of different ways to pray. Sometimes I kneel at my window with Mom. Sometimes I look up and lift my hands. I can sing a prayer. I can write or draw a prayer.

Whether my prayer is loud or quiet, God will hear it. Even though I can't see God's face, I know he is listening.

"The Lord listens when I pray to him." Psalm 4:3

No matter where I am, or how I do it, I can pray . . . and God will always, always listen.

Never stop praying.
—1 Thessalonians 5:17

A Child's Book of Manners

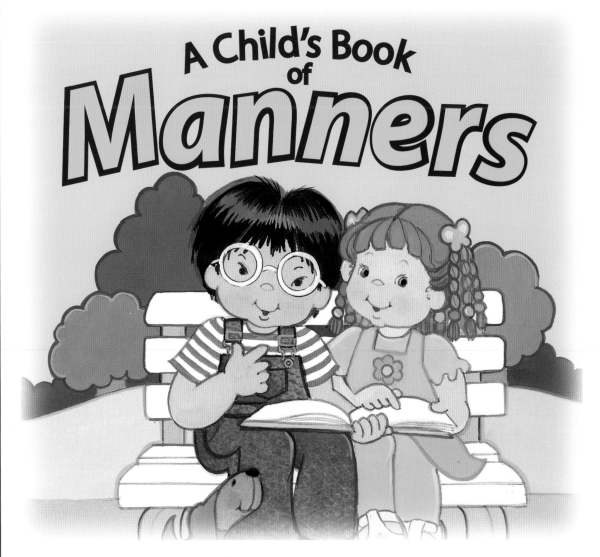

written by RUTH SHANNON ODOR

illustrated by JODIE MCCALLUM

Having good manners means being kind and thinking of others. From early in the morning till the end of the day, do and say things in the kindest way.

Good manners begin at home. Close the doors quietly. Walk—please do not run—in the house. Hang up your clothes. Put toys away.

At the table don't talk with your mouth full. If you want to leave the table, ask, "May I be excused?" If your mom or dad says yes, remember to say thank you.

Don't be a Shoveler Shawn, a Picky Pete, a Sarah the Slurper, or a Messy Bessie!

Cover your mouth when you cough, when you yawn, and when you sneeze.

Say please if you want something. Say thank you when you are given something. Say no, thank you when you do not want something.

If you want a friend, you have to be one. Take turns. Share. Play fair.

Don't be like Sulky Sue, Me-first Megan, Look-at-me Leo, or That's-mine Mark.

There are some very special rules to follow when you go to school. Walk—do not run—in the halls. Never push or shove. Help take care of the building and the playground.

Follow the rules. Obey the teacher. Be a good loser. Listen when others talk.

Be kind. Do not make fun of others. Do not brag—even if you are the best.

Be honest. Copying the answers may be the easy way, but it is not God's way. Always tell the truth—even when it is not easy.

When you go to church, try to be early. If you are late, sit near the back.

Do not whisper or giggle or talk. Do not rattle the pages of the songbook. When you disturb other people, they can't worship God.

Think about God. Sing to God. Pray to God. Listen to God's Word.

Jesus taught us to be kind, to love others, and to treat others as we would like to be treated. All these are good manners!

Jesus is God's Son. Jesus loves others more than himself.

If we try to be like Jesus in all we say and do, then having good manners will be as easy as . . . 1, 2, 3!

Helping Is Fun

written by ALICE GREENSPAN

illustrated by LINDA HOHAG

Helping makes us happy.
It adds sunshine to our days.
And even though we're little,
We can help in many ways.

I can rake the leaves with Grandpa.
I can help Mother bake a pie.
I can put my socks and sneakers on.
I can hunt for Dad's brown tie.

I can climb up high on a bedroom chair
And help mother zip her dress.
I can bathe my little brown puppy
When he's gotten in a mess.

I love to feed the goldfish
And help clean the family car.
My dog and I run to get the mail
'Long as Mother knows where we are.

I comb my hair and brush my teeth.
I even shine Gramps' old shoes.
I watch my baby sister,
And if I tickle her, she coos.

I can use a nice clean tissue
When my nose begins to run.
I can water plants
And fold my pants
Because helping can be fun.

I love to pick blueberries,
So Mother can make a dessert.
And I put my own little bandage on
When my knee begins to hurt.

I help my dad when he mows the yard;
Then he hugs me extra hard.
And I know when I help others
That I'm really helping God.

My Sister is Special

written by LARRY JANSEN

illustrated by ROBERT PEPPER

Hi. My name's Nathan. I like tacos, my hamster, and cartoons on Saturday morning. I don't like kissing on TV, Chinese food, or when my sister messes up my toys. But I like my sister.

She's special.

This is my sister, Rachel. She likes being "mommy" to all her dolls, going to our brother Matthew's house, pretending she is a newscaster, hugging, and helping our younger brother, Andrew. She doesn't like walking barefoot on hot pavement, riding horses, or getting her face wet.

Each of us has different likes and dislikes because each person is special. God made us all special, so we are all different.

We are short or tall, skinny or not so skinny, old or young or in-between. God made my sister special but in a different way.

Some kids are special because they are really smart. Some kids are special because they are really famous. Some kids are special because they run fast or throw a ball far.

Some kids are special because they have physical problems and need wheelchairs, or they are blind and need canes. My sister is special because she has Down syndrome. She learns slowly and needs special education.

I asked my dad how Rachel got Down syndrome. He said, "Your whole body is made up of tiny cells. Each of those cells is made up of chromosomes. You have 46 chromosomes in each cell. There are 23 from your father and 23 from your mother. But your sister somehow got an extra chromosome, so she has Down syndrome."

It takes Rachel a long time to learn some things that I learn quickly, like eating and drinking, walking and running, thinking and talking. She can walk, but it took her a long time to learn how. She can talk but not very well.

There are lots of people with disabilities. Some people have Down syndrome like Rachel. Some

people have other kinds of disabilities.

Sometimes we stare at them, and maybe we don't know what to say or do when we see them. But we can be their friends. Don't make fun of them or their disability. Remember God made them, and they are special like you and me.

God wants us to be good helpers, but I know there are lots of things people with Down syndrome can do for themselves.

If Rachel is having trouble, I can ask her if she needs help, but sometimes the best help is to let her do it herself. Every kid needs the chance to do things on her own.

My sister is fun to play with. She wants to do the things I do, so I try to do good things. I can't imagine my family without Rachel.

I learn things from Rachel too. She doesn't care what people look like or where they live. Rachel will be anyone's friend— no matter what.

Mostly, Rachel teaches me about love. She shows me that God loves us all no matter what.

I love my sister. My sister is special!

I'm Glad I'm Me!

written by FRANCES CARFI MATRANGA

illustrated by JODI MCCALLUM

I'm glad I'm not a busy ant just working all the day.
To work is good, but what about a little time to play?

I'm glad I'm not a kitten who *meows* for everything.
I like to talk and whisper; I like to hum and sing.

I'm glad I'm not a turtle with my house stuck onto me.
I couldn't hop and skip and run or climb up in a tree.

I'm glad I'm not a pack rat that hoards all kinds of junk.
And I'm glad that I am not a stinky little skunk!

I'm glad I'm not a penguin in a land of snow and ice;
With no trees or grass or flowers that smell so very nice.

I'm glad I'm not an owl that flies only at night
And has to sleep in daytime. Oh, no! I like the light.

I'm glad I'm not a dolphin living in the sea.
I'd have to swim and swim and SWIM—
          how tiring that would be.

I'm glad I'm not a tiger. Raw meat is all I'd eat.
No fruit or cake or ice cream—I'd get no special treat.

I'm glad I'm not a camel with a funny-looking hump
And a face that isn't friendly. Is a camel just a grump?

I'm glad I'm not a tall giraffe without a scarf and coat.
If I caught cold inside my neck, I'd have a HUGE sore throat!

I'm glad I'm not a crocodile with a scary, toothy grin.
I wouldn't like to be all green with bumpy, scaly skin.

I'm really glad that I'm a kid. It's what I want to be.
I'm glad to have my mom and dad—I'm GLAD God
made me, ME!

JESUS is my SPECIAL FRIEND

written by SUSAN S. BALIKA

illustrated by VICKEY BOLLING

I have a friend. His name is Zach.

Zach and I like to talk to each other. We wonder where clouds come from. We plan rocket trips to the moon. We share drippy ice cream.

But sometimes Zach goes shopping with his mother. Sometimes he goes to visit his grandparents. When we can't play together, I feel lonely.

I had another friend. Her name is Jamie.

Jamie and I liked to look at books and tell stories about the pictures. We liked to color with bright crayons. Sometimes our mothers put our drawings on the refrigerator.

One day a moving van came. The moving men put Jamie's books and crayons into brown boxes. They took down her swing set. Jamie moved away to another city. I miss her.

I have another friend. His name is David.

David and I like to play games together. We build roads in the sand and make garages from blocks. We pretend that David is the mechanic, and I am a racecar driver. Sometimes we fight. We get angry with each other. David takes his big yellow dump truck and goes home. That makes me feel sad inside. It is hard to say "I'm sorry."

But I have a very special friend. He never makes me feel lonely. He never moves away. He never goes home because he is angry with me. He is always with me even though I can't see him.

He is with me when I lie on my back in the tickly green grass and look up at the clouds.

He is with me when I toss leaves high in the air and jump in the falling colors.

He is with me when I whoosh down the hill in the crunchy snow.

He is with me because he wants to be with me.

When I've done something wrong, he lets me say "I'm sorry."

Jesus is my special friend. He loves me. He also loves Zach and Jamie and David. And he loves you! Jesus loves everybody.

Yes, Jesus is my special friend. He can be your special friend too.

WHAT IS LOVE?

written by SARAH EBERLE
illustrated by TAMMIE L. SPEER

Love is . . . *not* touching the eggs in a robin's nest . . . letting a butterfly go free . . . putting a tiny turtle back into the water.

Love is doing something to help other people.

Love is leaving the flowers for others to enjoy. Love is feeding the birds when they are hungry.

Love is visiting a sick friend. Love is inviting a new neighbor to come play with you.

Love is planning a special surprise for someone.

Love is helping Grandma bake cookies or giving her a cold drink.

Love is waiting for someone smaller to catch up.

Love is sharing your umbrella on a rainy day or helping someone find the way when it is dark.

Sometimes . . . you can show love by just being there when you are needed or by helping with a job that's too hard for only one person.

Love is kissing away the tears when someone is hurt and remembering to say, "I'm sorry."

Love is helping your little brother learn the alphabet or letting your little sister help, even when it would be easier to do it by yourself.

Love is doing something for others *because God loves you!*

Stories About
Values

"Be Patient" taken from

Buzzy Bee

STORY BOOK

written by RUTH CRANDALL
illustrated by VERA GOHMAN

"**W**ait!" cried Todd. "I'll go with you to the ballpark, but I have to run home for a minute. I'll be right back."

Jack waited with his bat over his shoulder. *Don't know why I should wait for him. I'm late now. Todd does like to play ball, though. Anyway, in Bible school we learned the verse,* Be patient toward all men. *I guess it won't hurt me to wait for Todd.*

Soon Todd came back.

"Thanks for waiting, Jack. Mom had to take my brother to the doctor, so I took my little sister to Grandma's for her nap. I know I made you late. I'm sorry."

"That's OK," smiled Jack. "Buzzy Bee says, 'Be patient.'"

"That's right," answered Todd. "Mom always tells me that Jesus wants me to be patient. I sure have to be patient with my little sister. But I love her, and I love Jesus too."

Good Habits for God's Kids
My Clean Room

written by JEAN FISCHER

illustrated by ANGELA KAMSTRA

"**S**ara Beth, your room's a mess!" Mom said when she tucked Sara Beth into bed. "Please have your room clean by tomorrow afternoon."

Sara Beth looked around her room at all her favorite things: her stuffed animals, her dolls, her books, her toys. She didn't think her room was messy.

The next morning Howard came over to play.

"Hey, Sara Beth," Howard said, "Let's ride our bikes to the park."

But Sara Beth couldn't find her bike helmet. She looked under her bed and inside her closet. She looked in her toy chest and under a pile of clothes. She looked on the bookcase and behind the door.

Sara Beth couldn't find her bike helmet, so she didn't go to the park with Howard.

Later that morning Oscar asked to borrow Sara Beth's goggles for his swimming lesson. But Sara Beth couldn't find her goggles. She looked under her bed and inside her closet. She looked in her toy chest and under a pile of clothes. Sara Beth looked on the bookcase and behind the door.

Sara Beth couldn't find her goggles, so she couldn't share with Oscar. She felt sorry about that.

Later that day Sara Beth heard the ice-cream truck coming down the street!

"Mom!" Sara Beth cried. "Can I have money for ice cream?"

"Look in your piggy bank," Mom answered.

Mom came in and sat down on the bed. "You're not a mess, sweetheart, but you are unhappy. God has given you so many good gifts—toys, games, books—but if you can't find them, you can't enjoy them or share them. When you take good care of your things, you please God, and you will be happier too."

But Sara Beth couldn't find her piggy bank. She looked under her bed and inside her closet. She looked in her toy chest and under a pile of clothes. She looked on the bookcase and behind the door. She even looked inside an empty box of crackers.

All of Sara Beth's friends got ice cream. But Sara Beth couldn't find her piggy bank, so Sara Beth didn't get any at all.

Sara Beth flopped down on her bed. She looked around her room and cried, "My room is a terrible mess, and so am I!"

Sara Beth stood up. She knew just what to do to please God and make herself happy.

First she cleaned under her bed. That's where she found her bike helmet.

Then Sara Beth hung up all her clothes. That's when she found her swimming goggles.

After that Sara Beth picked up all of her books and all of her toys.

And that's when she found her piggy bank!

"Mom!" Sara Beth called, "Come look at my clean room!"

"Now your room looks so much better, and so do you, Sara Beth. Thank you for taking care of your things and for obeying me today by cleaning up."

Then Sara Beth and her mom went together to find the ice-cream truck to celebrate Sara Beth's clean room.

Good Job, Rob!

written by JENNIFER STEWART
illustrated by NANCY MUNGER

Rob bounced up and down in the backseat as his dad pulled into the driveway of Uncle Ralph's farm.

"Hey, Will!" Rob called. "I'm ready to play on the swings and fish in the pond."

"Aren't you here to pick apples?" Will asked.

"Pick apples?" Rob said in surprise. "That's work! I came to play, like last time we were here."

"Today is a work day," Rob's mom explained. "It's time to harvest the apples from the orchard, and we all came to help."

"Maybe we can go fishing after our work is done," Will said.

Rob followed Will and Uncle Ralph to the apple orchard. "I don't want to pick apples," Rob said.

"You don't have to help, but you'll be missing out," Uncle

He slid down the slide all by himself.

He swung on the swings all by himself.

He played fetch with the dog all by himself.

Finally, he flopped down beside the pond and watched the frogs jumping from log to log. *It's not much fun to play all by myself,* he thought. *Maybe playing alone while everyone is working isn't such a good idea.*

He remembered what Uncle Ralph had told him: *It feels good to work hard and do a good job, and the Bible says, "You will produce fruit in every good work."* Suddenly Rob jumped up and ran to the orchard.

"Can I help you?" Rob asked Uncle Ralph.

"Of course you can!" said Uncle Ralph. "I am so glad you decided to join us. We can always use another hard worker. In fact, I need someone to deliver these apples to Grandpa right away. He's making apple cider."

Ralph said. "It feels good to work hard and do a good job, and in Colossians 1:10, the Bible says, 'You will produce fruit in every good work.'"

Rob looked at the rows and rows of apple trees. The orchard was great for a picnic in the shade or a game of hide-and-seek—but not for work!

"I don't want to pick apples," Rob said again. "I'm going to play." So Rob went off by himself.

Rob visited the barn cats all by himself.

Rob walked through the orchard. The big bucket wasn't too heavy for him!

"Thanks, Rob. Good job!" said Grandpa when he saw Rob and the bucket of apples. A big smile flashed on Rob's face. He rushed back to Uncle Ralph to get more apples.

"This basket is for Will to load on the truck to take to the market," said Uncle Ralph.

Rob hurried to the truck with the full basket.

"Thanks, Rob. Good job!" said Will as he loaded the basket.

Uncle Ralph was right! It did feel good to do a good job!

The rest of the day, Rob delivered apples from the orchard to places all over the farm. He skipped across the yard. He cut through the barn. He walked down the cellar steps.

He marched up the porch steps into the big kitchen.

"Thanks, Rob. Good job!" said Grandma. "You're just in time for me to make more apple turnovers."

When all the apples were picked and supper was over, everyone gathered around a cozy campfire to rest a while and enjoy Grandma's apple turnovers.

"I'm sorry we didn't get to go fishing," Will said.

"That's OK," Rob said. "It feels good to work hard. And just like the Bible verse said, look at all the fruit I produced!"

"Good job, Rob!" Uncle Ralph said. "But that Bible verse wasn't talking about apples. Producing fruit means doing the good things God wants us to do. You pleased God with the way you helped us today."

Rob smiled and took a bite of his turnover. He was glad he had done a good job.

Good Habits for God's Kids
Good for You

written by LAURA DERICO

illustrated by ANGELA KAMSTRA

"**B**russels sprouts? Green beans? Spinach? Broccoli?! DAD?!?" Oscar shouted.

"Where is all the *good* food?" Oscar asked, peering into the refrigerator.

"This food *is* good, Oscar—it's good for you! God gave us healthy bodies, and we need to take better care of them by eating healthy foods and exercising," Dad said.

"Maybe it's good for *you*, but I don't need that stuff—I'm young! Besides, eating green things all the time and doing chin-ups is boring," Oscar whined.

"OK, Oscar, for the next week, you can eat what you want and not exercise. What do you say?" Oscar's dad asked.

"I say that's great! Wait till my friends find out!" Oscar said happily.

When Howard and Sara Beth came over later, they were thrilled to see the table full of all their favorite goodies. The three friends stuffed their mouths with Cheesy Fluff, Sugar Sticks, and Coco-Chews. They slurped up soda pop and chomped up chips.

They slouched on the couch, flopped on the floor, and became blobs on the beanbag chairs. They ate so much they couldn't even move!

After five video games and three bags of snacks, it was time for Howard and Sara Beth to go home. "Wow, Oscar, that was yummy, but I sure do feel funny," said Howard, rubbing his tummy.

"*Yawwwnnn!* I'm so sleepy! If I ate like that every day, I'd never make it through the church picnic race next month," Sara Beth said.

"Well, I love to eat whatever I want. I know I'll make it through that race—I might even win!" Oscar replied.

The next morning Oscar slept late and skipped breakfast. When he finally got up, Dad was already dressed in his jogging clothes. "Would you like to exercise with me today, Oscar?" Dad asked.

"No way!" Oscar said. "I don't need any exercise. Besides, I'm going to Sara Beth's house today."

Oscar had fun with Sara Beth and his other friends all afternoon until they decided to run relay races. Oscar ran as fast as he could, but he lost every time. Even little Simon, who was only 4, beat him. So Oscar trudged home and had cold pizza and ice cream for dinner.

The next day Oscar had a big bowl of Sugar Poofs for breakfast. "Sure you don't want to exercise with me today?" Dad asked.

Oscar said, "No way! I don't need any exercise. I'm going to play at Howard's house."

At Howard's house everybody swam laps in the pool to see who could do the most in five minutes. Oscar paddled and splashed, but he could do only one lap. Even little Simon did three! Oscar sloshed home and ate another bowl of Sugar Poofs.

The next day Oscar and his dad walked to meet Oscar's friends at the bottom of Big Hill. "So no exercise again today, Oscar?" Dad asked.

"No way, Dad! I told you I don't need that stuff. I'm just going to play with my friends," Oscar grumped. His head hurt and he felt very grouchy. Oscar ate a candy bar as he waited for his friends.

All the friends climbed up Big Hill, but Oscar didn't get halfway up before he had to rest. He huffed, puffed, and plopped down on the ground. Then he watched as all of the rest of his friends—even that little Simon!—cheered when they reached the top. Oscar just sighed, stumbled back down the hill, and shuffled home.

Oscar was thirsty and hungry, but none of his soda or snacks looked good. "What's wrong, Oscar?" Dad asked.

"Dad, I'm a loser! I'm so slow, and I get so tired. Even Simon is faster than I am! I'll never win that church race now," Oscar said, slumping on the couch.

"Oscar, you're no loser. God designed our bodies, and he's also provided the food to help them do what they need to do. But there is something we need to do too," Dad said.

"You mean start eating green things and doing chin-ups?" Oscar asked.

"Not exactly," Dad smiled.

The next day Oscar's dad made a delicious breakfast. "You mean this is good for me?" Oscar asked.

"Yes, Oscar, green vegetables are good, but there are all kinds of foods you can and should eat to keep your body healthy—foods that taste great!" his dad said.

After breakfast they played soccer in the yard. "You mean this is exercise?" Oscar asked, bouncing a ball on his knee.

"Yep, that's right," Dad said. "Exercise isn't just doing chin-ups. In fact, you have been exercising all week when you were playing with your friends. But you still need to exercise regularly and keep doing activities that will help your muscles stretch and grow—things that you like to do!"

Oscar started doing a little exercise every day. He practiced soccer kicks, skated at the park, and swam laps at the pool. He had fun running races and jumping rope with his pals. Three times a week, Oscar jogged with his dad. Then they raced to see who could do the most sit-ups. Oscar even had fun doing chin-ups!

Oscar's dad also helped him learn how to eat better—and not just green things! They ate balanced meals with good foods full of vitamins and nutrients. Oscar learned to look for healthy food at the supermarket instead of just grabbing stuff full of sugar and fat. Oscar and his dad enjoyed treats every once in a while, but Oscar even started to like the sweet taste of apples and berries better than sugary snacks.

When the Sunday of the race finally arrived, Oscar felt strong, healthy, and very happy! Oscar listened in church as missionaries told about kids in other countries who were sick and had little food.

Oscar prayed, "God, thank you for giving me a healthy body and good food and water every day. Help me to take care of my body and to help others be healthy too."

Before the race Oscar made sure to eat an energy-filled lunch and to drink lots of water. Then he joined his friends at the starting line and stretched his arms and legs. They all waited for the signal. *BANG!* They were off—and Oscar was in the lead!

Oscar's dad waited for him at the finish line. Several of Oscar's friends finished and waited too. Where was Oscar?

Finally, Oscar appeared—carrying little Simon on his back! They crossed the finish line and, while Oscar caught his breath, Simon explained, "I tripped and hurt my foot, but Oscar helped me. He was able to carry me all the way to the end of the race!"

"Well, son, you may not have won the race, but you sure are a winner. What if we celebrate with some ice cream and strawberries?" Dad asked.

"Thanks, Dad, but I'll just take the strawberries," Oscar smiled. "You know, they're good for you!"

Be Brave, Anna!

written by
JODEE MCCONNAUGHHAY
illustrated by **JILL DUBIN**

The room was quiet. The window was dark. The night-light made shadows dance on the wall.

Anna was tucked snugly in her bed, a soft pillow under her head. She was very, *very*, sleepy.

So why were Anna's eyes wide open?

"Daddy!" Anna cried and ducked under her soft quilt.

"What's wrong?" Daddy asked, coming quickly into the room.

"I'm afraid," Anna said, peeping out at her father's face.

Sitting on the bed, Daddy held Anna's hand and said, "Do

you know what I say when *I'm* afraid?"

Daddy never seems afraid, Anna thought. So she sat up and asked, "What do you say when you're afraid?"

"When I'm afraid, I always say, The Lord is my helper; I will not be afraid," Daddy said. "Now say it with me and you will see."

"The Lord is my helper; I will not be afraid," they said.

"I like it," Anna said, hugging her knees to her chest, "but how does it help?"

"It reminds us that God is always with us," Daddy said. "And with such a big, strong helper, we don't need to stay afraid."

Daddy makes me feel safe, Anna thought. *And God is even bigger than Daddy!*

"So," Daddy asked, "what will you say when you are afraid in your bed?"

"The Lord is my helper; I will not be afraid," Anna said.

"And when you see the doctor because you are sick?"

"I'll say it quickly—The Lord is my helper; I will not be afraid," Anna said.

"And when Bethany's big dog runs over to play?"

"Then I will say—The Lord is my helper; I will not be afraid," Anna said.

"And when Nathaniel's cat swats your foot as you walk by, will you cry?"

"No, I'll reply—The Lord is my helper; I will not be afraid," Anna said.

"But what if the thunder is crashing, the lightning is flashing, and the rain is splashing outside your window here? What will you say then, my dear?"

Anna snuggled in her bed and said, "Daddy, I will say loud and clear—The Lord is my helper; I will not be afraid!"

Daddy smiled, kissed Anna's cheek, and stepped softly from the room.

The room was quiet. The window was dark. The night-light made shadows dance on the purple wall.

Tucked snugly in her warm bed, a soft pillow under her head, Anna knew—God was with her too.

So she smiled, closed her sleepy eyes, and said, "The Lord is my helper, I . . . will . . . not . . . be . . . afraid." Hebrews 13:6

Lost in the Store

written by CLARE MISHICA

illustrated by JILL DUBIN

"This is a big store," Mama said. "Stay close."

"We will," said Samantha. She whirled and twirled around with Bear. Bear went everywhere with Samantha.

Mama looked at dresses. She picked up a bright red dress with a purple scarf. Samantha whirled and twirled some more. She spun around the dress racks until she was very dizzy.

"Oh, no," said Samantha as she stopped spinning and sat down on the floor. "I think I left Bear in the garden department!"

Samantha looked over her shoulder. *Mama told me to stay close, but I'll only be gone a minute,* she thought. She hurried back to the garden department.

There was Bear, right where she'd left him! Samantha skipped back to the dresses with Bear. "Here we are!" she giggled. But Mama wasn't there.

"Mama?" Samantha called. She ran down one aisle and up

another, but she still did not see her mother. "I think we're lost," she told Bear, and she gave him a hug. "Don't worry. We'll find Mama."

Samantha saw someone wearing a yellow skirt. "Mama is wearing a yellow skirt," Samantha said to Bear. "Maybe that's Mama." Samantha and Bear hurried down the aisle. But the lady wearing the yellow skirt had gray curls and a flowery bag. "That's not Mama," said Samantha.

Samantha spotted someone wearing a hat with red flowers. "That looks like Mama's hat," Samantha told Bear. They ran down the aisle to look. But the lady wearing the hat had a stroller and a baby. The baby waved at Samantha and Bear. "That's not Mama," Samantha said as she walked by. "Where could Mama be?"

Samantha's stomach felt like she'd swallowed a roller coaster. Hot tears slipped down Samantha's cheeks. They dripped on Bear and on the shiny floor. "Dear God," Samantha prayed. "I'm scared and I can't find my Mama."

Then Samantha remembered a song Mama had taught her.

She sang to Bear, "If you're lost in a store, what do you do? Ask a friendly store clerk, and she'll help you. March to the cash register—one, two, three. Don't be afraid. Clerks can find your family."

"God helped me remember Mama's song," Samantha told Bear. "Now I know what to do! I'll be brave and ask for help. Don't worry. You won't have to talk." Samantha wiped her tears and walked up to the front of the store.

"Hello," said Samantha in a wobbly voice to the clerk behind the cash register. "Can you help me and Bear find my mother?"

The clerk smiled and took her hand. "Sure I can," she said. "Let's go to the service desk. They'll make an announcement that everyone in the store will hear. What's your name?"

"My name is Samantha Baker," said Samantha. "And this is Bear."

From the service desk, a big voice over the loudspeaker said, "Would Mrs. Baker please report to the service desk? Samantha is waiting for you. Mrs. Baker, please report to the service desk. Thank you."

Samantha smiled a little smile. "Now Mama will know where to find us," she told Bear. Samantha sat with Bear and waited.

Soon a happy voice said, "Samantha!" It was Mama's voice. Samantha jumped off her chair and into her mother's arms. She gave her mother a giant hug, and her mother hugged her back. "I'm so glad I found you," said Mama. "Why didn't you stay with me?"

"I'm really sorry," Samantha said. "Bear and I are going to stay very close to you now."

"That's good," said Mama.

Then she gave Samantha and Bear another hug, and Samantha smiled the happiest and biggest smile of all.

Good Habits for God's Kids
TV Time~Out

written by LAURA SHIPP CLARKE AND DAVE SHIPP
illustrated by ANGELA KAMSTRA

Howard sank into a pile of comfy pillows and settled in for another Saturday in front of the TV.

"Looks like a beautiful day out," said Dad. "Why don't you go play outside for a change?"

"No way!" Howard said. "I don't want to miss cartoons."

Click. Click. Howard pushed the buttons of the TV remote control.

Click. Click. Click. But nothing happened!

"Dad! Something's wrong with the TV!"

Dad looked at the remote control. "I think this just needs some new batteries," he said.

"Well, aren't you going to fix it?" Howard asked.

"I don't know," said Dad. "Our family spends a lot of time watching TV—maybe too much. This might be a good chance for us to take a TV time-out."

"That's a good idea!" said Mom. "Think about all the good things we could do with our time."

"But I can't miss all my favorite shows!" Howard wailed.

"I think we should try it," Dad insisted. "Just for this week, our TV will stay off."

Howard slumped down on the porch steps. He was bored already. "With no TV there's nothing to do!" he said.

"Hey, Howard!" Sara Beth called out as she rode up the sidewalk on her bike. "I'm on my way to play kickball in Oscar's yard. Do you want to come?"

"I guess so," Howard said. "I don't have anything better to do. My family is taking a TV time-out." Howard got his bike and went with Sara Beth to join the kickball game.

Once the game had started, Howard didn't think at all about his favorite TV shows. He was too busy tagging out runners and racing around the bases.

After the kickball game, everyone decided to go to Sara Beth's house to build a fort.

"How was your day?" Mom asked at bedtime.

"I had a blast!" Howard said. "We played kickball and made a fort. Later we're going to turn the fort into a castle and make a dragon. We might even put on a play!"

"I guess you found something to do even without TV," said Dad. Then they made plans for all the things they would do as a family during the TV time-out.

In Sunday school the next day, Oscar and Sara Beth asked Howard if he and his family would like to help with the car wash later that afternoon. "We wash someone's car for free, and then we tell that person 'God loves you.'" Oscar explained.

Usually, Howard wanted to stay home to watch movies and play video games, but today he said, "Sure, I'll help! Let me ask my dad."

Howard had a great time scrubbing tires, washing windows, and getting splashed with soap. He washed lots of cars, and he talked to 17 people about God's love!

Howard played soccer on Monday. On Tuesday he played trains at Sara Beth's house. Wednesday his family collected canned goods for the church food drive. On Thursday Howard won his family's checkers tournament.

On Friday Dad took the family out for pizza.

"I've enjoyed the family time we have had this week," Mom said.

"And I'm glad we didn't miss out on the car wash Sunday," Howard said.

"Or the church food drive," Dad added.

On Saturday Mom bought new batteries for the remote. The TV time-out was officially over.

Later that evening Dad said, "The Mysterious Detective show is coming on, Howard. Do you want to watch it with me?"

"Maybe another time," said Howard. "Let's have one more night of TV time-out. I challenge you to a checkers rematch!"

Cody's New Friends

written by CLARE MISHICA

illustrated by STEPHANIE BRITT

I wanted to hit a home run over the birdhouses and into the woods, so I practiced and practiced. But during our first camp ball game, I only hit a double. I raced to second base.

Next, Dan came up to bat. He hit the ball with a *smack* and I ran to third base, but Dan tripped over a little rock when he ran. Dan probably would trip over an ant.

"Good try," said Counselor Joe.

"Allie's turn to bat," Counselor Joe said.

Allie struck out. I bet she couldn't even see the ball. Her super-thick glasses are always sliding down her nose.

"You'll hit it the next time," Counselor Joe said. He says nice stuff like that to everybody.

Thomas was our last hope for a hit. He looked big enough to hit the ball halfway around the world, but he struck out too.

"Oh no," our team groaned, and we lost the game.

After our ball game, we went for a hike. I found two pinecones, a rock shaped like a hippopotamus, and a lucky penny. I looked back and Dan, Allie, and Thomas were walking slower than sleepy snails.

"What a bunch of slowpokes!" I heard someone whisper.

"They're so weird!" another person giggled.

"Come on," Counselor Joe called to Dan, Thomas, and Allie. "You can catch up."

After our hike we made clay pots. Mine looked like a shoe.

"Wow! How did you do that?" a girl asked.

"I accidentally sat on it," I said with a smile.

Dan, Thomas, and Allie sat at a table in the corner. Nobody talked to them at all.

On the second day of camp, everyone played ball again. First, I struck out. Then when I was in the outfield, the ball went flying over

150

my head and into the bushes. I found the ball, and some bees found me!

Bzzzzz! The bees swarmed around my head.

I got scared and ran, and the bees stung me three times. My cheeks felt like two pincushions full of sharp needles.

Counselor Joe put ice on the bee stings. "This should help," he said.

Finally, my cheeks stopped hurting, but my face was red and lumpy.

The other campers were making pictures using glue and colored sand. When I walked into the room, they stared at me. The only empty chair was in the corner by Dan, Thomas, and Allie.

"What a funny face!" I heard someone whisper.

"He's weird!" another person giggled loudly.

I wanted to shout at the campers. I wanted to say, "I don't care if you laugh at me! I don't care if you don't like me!"

But I really did care. I sat next to Dan, and I wondered if he felt the same way. He knocked over the blue sand, and it landed on the head of the spider I was making.

"Sorry," mumbled Dan. He tried to clean up the mess.

"It's OK," I told him. "That can be the sky."

"It looks more like a giant blueberry," Dan said.

"Hey, that's a great idea," I said. "I'll make my spider right in the middle of a blueberry patch."

When I finished, Counselor Joe held up my picture for everyone to see because it looked so neat. I gave Dan a high five.

Next, we went into the pool. No one swam with me except Dan, Thomas, and Allie.

"Let's play catch," Thomas said. He had a red ball.

After our ball game Thomas showed Allie, Dan, and me how to twirl a ball on our fingers. Then we tried twirling the ball on our noses, and I laughed so hard I got the hiccups.

After swimming we practiced a song we were learning to sing for our parents. No one made room for me to stand except Dan, Thomas, and Allie.

Allie clapped her hands while we sang. *Clappity, clap. Clappity clap!* I started to clap too.

"That's a great beat, Allie," Counselor Joe told us. "We will call it the 'Allie Beat.'"

That night we had a hot dog roast. My face was still all red and puffy. No one would sit next to me except Dan, Thomas, and Allie. After we ate Counselor Joe told us a Bible story about Jesus.

"Jesus loves us very much," Counselor Joe said. "He wants us to love everyone, even people who look or act differently from us. You can show Jesus' love by including others in your games, by speaking kindly, and by being friendly. Loving everyone isn't really that hard to do. It just takes a little practice."

I thought about those words that night. *How could I show love to everyone?* I wondered.

The next morning only one tiny red spot was left on my cheek. When I got to camp, it was time to play ball, and no one stared at me anymore.

"Come on, Cody, be on our team," someone called. But I saw Dan, Thomas, and Allie standing all by themselves. I remembered how sad I felt when the other kids wouldn't play with me.

Then I remembered what Jesus said about loving everyone, and how fun it was to play with Dan, Thomas, and Allie. *It's not so hard to love others,* I thought. *And maybe I could do it even better if I practiced and practiced.*

"Come on," I called to Dan, Thomas, and Allie. "You can be on our team too."

Dan, Thomas, and Allie walked over, and at first, no one said anything. Then Counselor Joe shouted, "Play ball!" and everyone started laughing and playing together.

That day I hit my very first home run.

"This is my command: Love each other as I have loved you." —John 15:12

"Be Thankful" taken from

Buzzy Bee Says,
"BEE HAPPY"

written by BARBARA CURIE
illustrated by RUSSELL RIGO

Susan Smith was thankful and at the end of the day, she always knelt beside her bed and then to God she'd say: "Thank you for the nicest day I think I've ever had. Thank you for my home and for my mom and dad.

"I'm thankful for my country and for the freedom here. I've heard about some places where the people live in fear.

"Thank you, God, for Jesus and for the Bible too. Thank you for my teachers, who help me learn of you."

Always give thanks to God the Father for everything, in the name of our Lord Jesus Christ. —Ephesians 5:20

Keep Trying, Travis!

written by JODEE MCCONNAUGHHAY
illustrated by STEPHEN CARPENTER

Travis pedaled. His bike took off in a flash. Then it started to wobble, then lean, and then . . .

CRASH!!

"I can't!" Travis cried, getting up off the ground. He threw off his helmet and stomped all around.

"What's the problem?" asked Dad, running out through the door.

"I can't ride my bike!" Travis pouted some more.

"Oh, I don't mean all the clutter and clatter. Something far worse than that is the matter. Stop saying, 'I can't.' It will not do. With practice and prayer, God can help you. You must remember what the Bible says, 'I can do everything through him who gives me strength.'"

Travis asked his dad, "But why does God care if I ride my bike? What does it matter to him what I like to do?"

"God loves us and helps us with big things or small. He wants us to trust him with anything at all. Pretend you are trying with all your might but can't make a puzzle piece fit just right. What should you recite?"

"'I can do everything through him who gives me strength.'"

"Yes!" said Dad. "And when you stay overnight at Zach's but miss your home and want to come back, what is it you should say?"

"'I can do everything through him who gives me strength.'"

"Right!" said Dad. "And if the new boy needs a friend, but you're afraid to talk to him. What is it you should think?"

"'I can do everything through him who gives me strength.'"

"Right!" said Dad. "And if you have trouble reading your book, should you close it up quicklyv without taking a look? No! Instead what should you say?"

"'I can do everything through him who gives me strength.'"

"Right!" said Dad. "And when you swing a little too late to hit the ball as it crosses the plate, what is it you should say?

"'I can do everything through him who gives me strength.'"

"Good!" said Dad. "Now if you ride your bike a bit but wobble or wreck and want to quit, what is it you will think?"

"'I can do everything through him who gives me strength.'"

"Great! You know, Travis, many things are hard to do. It takes time to learn something new. But you won't have to work alone when you ask God's help all along."

Travis looked at the bike laying there, then closed his eyes and said a prayer.

"Lord, help me learn not to give in if something's hard when I begin. I know you'll give me the strength I need, so I will try until I succeed."

Then grabbing his helmet, Travis said with a grin, "With God's help, I can try again and again and again! 'I can do everything through him who gives me strength.'"

I can do everything through him who gives me strength. —*Philippians 4:13*

Don't Do That, Dexter!

written by JODEE MCCONNAUGHHAY
illustrated by RICHARD MAX KOLDING

Running, jumping, through the house,
seems like fun, you see.
But Mommy says, "Don't do that, Dexter!
Outside's the place to be."
Running, jumping, through the house,
I slipped and skinned my knee.
Mommy washed and bandaged it,
and kissed me on the cheek.
Obey your parents in the Lord, for this is right!

Clinging to Mom's bedpost high,
I'm a monkey on a tree.
Then this monkey's Mom came in, and said,
"Climb down to me!"
Clinging to the bedpost high, my shirt got stuck on top.
Mommy had to lift me off—my neck hurt quite a lot!
Obey your parents in the Lord, for this is right!

Driving, dumping, digging deep,
I make trucks bump and roar.
Then Daddy said, "It's time for a snack—
when your trucks are off the floor."
Driving, dumping, digging deep,
I bumped and roared some more.
Then Mommy said, "No snack tonight—
I see trucks still on the floor."
Obey your parents in the Lord, for this is right!

Swinging on the curtains, a super hero—whee!
'Til Daddy said, "Now that's enough.
It's time to go to sleep."
Swinging on the curtains caused such a mess for Dad.
When they crumpled to the floor, it really made him sad.
Obey your parents in the Lord, for this is right!

Bouncing on my bed at night, a spaceman on the moon.
But Daddy says this astronaut should settle down real soon.
Bouncing on my bed at night, I bounced right off the bed.
I cried and cried and Daddy came
with ice for my bumped head.
Obey your parents in the Lord, for this is right!

You don't have to tell me twice, I'm as smart as I can be.
When Mom and Dad say, "Don't do that!"
It's because they love me!

Children, obey your parents in the Lord, for this is right. —Ephesians 6:1

DON'T DO THAT, DEXTER

Tell the Truth, Tyler!

written by JODEE MCCONNAUGHHAY

illustrated by JACKIE URBANOVIC

Half an hour before supper, Dad put down his tools and stared hard at Tyler's face. "Did you eat chocolate cake?" he asked.

"No," said Tyler, blinking his eyes and biting his lip.

"Are you sure you didn't sneak a piece?" Dad asked.

Why does he keep asking? Tyler wondered.

Then Dad took Tyler to the hallway mirror. There Tyler saw two big brown eyebrows, two big brown blinking eyes, one set of chocolate-covered lips, and one chocolate-covered nose. Oops!!

"Now," Dad said, "did you eat chocolate cake when Mom told you to wait?"

Tyler looked at his feet. "Yes," he answered softly.

"Why didn't you tell me the truth?" Dad asked, gently wiping the chocolate from Tyler's nose.

"I was afraid to," Tyler said.

"You know," Dad said, "it's not always easy to tell the truth. But God says it's the right thing to do. The Bible says 'Stop telling lies. Tell each other the truth.' Even if it's hard to do, speak up and tell the truth."

"My teacher found gum on the floor and wondered who had the gum before. I felt bad and didn't tell it was mine. Is that a lie?" Tyler asked.

"Saying you did it is hard to do, but NOT speaking up is lying too. 'Stop telling lies. Tell each other the truth.' Even if you feel bad, speak up and tell the truth."

"If Mom makes me wear my itchy sweater, and I wear it now, but take it off later—Does Mom really need to know?" Tyler asked.

"When you try to fool someone, this too is a lie, my son. 'Stop telling lies. Tell each other the truth.' Don't be sneaky, speak up and tell the truth."

"Last week I bragged that I had a new ball, but I knew it wasn't new at all. Did I lie or was that just pretending?" Tyler asked.

"If you pretend to have more than you do, it's a lie to let folks believe that it's true. 'Stop telling lies. Tell each other the truth.' Don't make things up, speak up and tell the truth."

"When I wash my hands at school, but don't use soap, which is the rule, is it a lie if I say I washed my hands?"

"Half-truths are still lies, you see—lies that hide the truth from you and me. 'Stop telling lies. Tell each other the truth.' Don't hide in a lie, speak up and tell the truth."

"I drew in a book the other day, but no one noticed when I put it away. I won't get in trouble if no one knows," Tyler said.

"A lie is a lie no matter what, even if you don't get caught. 'Stop telling lies. Tell each other the truth.' God sees the truth anyway, so speak up and tell the truth."

Just then, Tyler's little sister skipped into the room. Dad stared hard at her face. "Did you cut your hair?" he asked.

"No," Sarah said in a wee little voice.

Here we go again, Tyler thought, as he looked from Sarah's safety scissors to her crooked cut curls. And Tyler and Dad together said,

"'Stop telling lies. Tell each other the truth.' Even when it's hard to do, speak up and tell the truth!"

So you must stop telling lies. Tell each other the truth. —Ephesians 4:25

Bear, Your Manners Are Showing

written by
KATHLEEN ALLAN MEYER

illustrated by
CREATIVE STUDIOS

Bear was eating a delicious blueberry cookie. He had taken it out of the cookie jar without asking.

"Goodness gracious, Little Bear," said his mother. "Where *have* your manners gone?"

Bear stopped munching. He turned around to look for his manners. "I don't see them in back of me," he answered.

"Manners aren't in back of you," said Mother Bear. "They are in your heart. I'll have to do something to help you remember them." So she went to her desk.

When she came back, Mother Bear had a purple inkpad and four little stamps. One at a time, she stamped them on a piece of paper.

"This one says please. When you want something, you say the magic word, *please*. This one says thank you. When someone gives you something, you always say the magic words *thank you*. This one says I'm sorry. When you do something that you shouldn't, you say the magic words *I'm sorry*. And this last one says excuse me. When someone is in your way, don't push them. You find the magic words *excuse me*."

"Now please let me have your four paws, Little Bear," Mother Bear said. Then *stamp! stamp! stamp! stamp!* And there were Little Bear's manners on his four little paws!

"Now off to school with you," Mother Bear said. But first she gave him a big bear hug.

In nursery school Little Bear saw two friends playing with a lovely lump of red clay. "I want some of that," he said to them. And he reached over to grab Teddy's piece.

"No, you can't have it," Teddy yelled.

As Little Bear raised his paw, he saw the magic word stamped on it, *please*.

"Please," he said softly. And Teddy put a big lump of the red clay in Little Bear's paw.

I think something comes next, Little Bear thought scratching his head. *What were those words?* Then he looked at his other paw. There were the two words he needed, *thank you*.

"Thank you, Teddy," Little Bear said. His friend smiled. Then Teddy handed an extra piece of red clay to Little Bear. *Mother Bear was right,* Little Bear said to himself, *these really are magic words!*

Soon it was time for outside play. Little Bear needed to go past two of his friends standing in the doorway. Maybe this was the time for more magic words. He looked at his other paw. There were the right words he could use!

"Excuse me," Little Bear said politely. And his two friends moved over as fast as you can say, "Jack Robinson."

Once Bear was outside, he ran toward the jungle gym. On the way he bumped into Bill Bear and knocked him down. Little Bear fell right on top of him. Bill Bear cried and rubbed the bump on his head. Then Little Bear raised is head and saw the stamp print on the bottom of his paw. "I'm sorry," it said.

Little Bear knew just what to do! He climbed off of Bill and then helped him get up. And, of course, he said, "Bill, I'm sorry."

Bill stopped crying and handed his blue car to Little Bear. Little Bear had always wanted to play with that car!

I'm sorry were magic words just like *please* and *thank you!*

The more Little Bear used *please* and *thank you* and *I'm sorry* and *excuse me*, the easier it was to remember them. After awhile he didn't need to look at his paws anymore.

And when the winter rains came and washed the magic words off his four little paws, Little Bear wasn't upset one bit. For by this time, they were in his heart— just like Mother Bear had hoped.

BEAR, YOUR MANNERS ARE SHOWING

Stories About
Holidays

THE VERY SPECIAL NIGHT

written by RUTH SHANNON ODOR

illustrated by PAT KARCH

Nights are for resting and sleeping. Some nights are quiet. Some nights are stormy. Some nights are dark. Some are bright with a big moon and twinkling stars. Most nights are just ordinary. But some are very special.

One night, a night long, long ago, was a special night—a very special night!

The town of Bethlehem was quiet that night. Almost everyone was asleep. In the stable of an inn slept a man and a woman. The man was Joseph and the woman was Mary. They had to sleep in the stable. When they had come to Bethlehem that day, they had found the inn crowded. In the same stable slept the cows and the donkeys.

During the night a wonderful thing happened! A baby was born to Mary. He was a special baby. He was the Son of God!

Mary wrapped the baby in soft clothes. Then she laid him on the soft hay in the manger.

"I will name you Jesus," Mary said.

It was a very special night—a very special night indeed!

That very same night, out on a hill near Bethlehem, shepherds were taking care of their sheep. To them this was the same kind of night as any other when they watched over their sheep and lambs.

Suddenly, a bright light shone around them! And a bright and shining angel stood before them!

"Do not be afraid," said the angel. "I bring you good news— good news for everyone.

"Tonight in the city of Bethlehem, the Savior, Christ the Lord, is born! You will find him wrapped in swaddling clothes and lying in a manger."

Then there were many angels praising God. They said, "Glory to God in the highest. And on earth peace, goodwill among men."

As quickly as they had come, the bright light and the angels were gone! Once more the night was dark and still. The shepherds were amazed.

"Let's go to Bethlehem," they said.

There they found Mary and Joseph and baby Jesus!

On the way home, the shepherds thanked God for what they had seen and heard that very special night.

At night in a land far way, some wise men were looking at the stars in the sky. They saw a big, new star! It meant God's Son was born!

How excited the wise men were! They planned a trip to the faraway land to find the baby, to worship him, and to give him gifts.

It was a very special night— that night long ago—when Jesus was born.

The Best Thing About Christmas

written by CHRISTINE HARDER TANGVALD

illustrated by CHERYL NOBENS

I like everything about Christmas, don't you?

I like to decorate our Christmas tree with silver tinsel, and pretty ornaments, and tiny lights that wink and blink, blink and wink. And I like to put shiny round balls on our Christmas tree—decorating our Christmas tree is fun.

But that's not the BEST thing about Christmas.

I like all of the colors of Christmas. Blue and green packages

tied with bows made of satin ribbon, and snowy white candles to light with a match, and bright yellow stars that twinkle and shine through the night, and striped red candy canes stuffed in our Christmas stockings.

Oh yes. I like the colors of Christmas. But that's not the BEST thing about Christmas.

I like all the special words we use at Christmas. "Ho, Ho, HO!" "Merry Christmas, everyone!" "JOY to the world!"

And I like all the things people do at Christmas to help other people. We care and share. We shake hands and smile and say, "Hello! How are you? It's so good to see you."

It makes me feel good when I care and share with other people. But that's not the BEST thing about Christmas.

I like all the good foods we eat at Christmas. Pretty sugar cookies with red and green frosting and sprinkles on the top. Yum, YUM, YUM!

And turkey with dressing and cranberry sauce and pumpkin pie with lots of whipped cream for dessert. Yum, YUM, **YUM!**

And big round oranges, and chocolate fudge, and gooey, chewy gumdrops! **YUM, YUM, YUM!**

I love gooey, chewy gumdrops! But that's not the BEST thing about Christmas.

I like the joyful sounds of Christmas. *DING, DONG, DING!* FA, la la la LA, la LA, LA, LA!

And I like the smells of Christmas. The fresh smell of our pine wreath hanging on the front door and the smell of Mom's apple pie baking in the oven. Mmmm. Mmmm. Good.

But that's still not the BEST thing about Christmas.

And I like the time we spend together during Christmas—eating together, praying together, reading together, shopping together, and just talking together.

Being together at Christmas is nice. But that's not the BEST thing about Christmas either!

Then what IS the best thing about Christmas?

I think the BEST thing about Christmas is . . . Jesus! Baby Jesus!

Yes, Jesus is the BEST thing about Christmas.

You see, Christmas is Jesus' birthday. And did you know that Jesus is God's own Son? He is. He is God's very own Son.

Long ago, baby Jesus was born in a stable in a little town called Bethlehem. Mary was Jesus' mother. Joseph was there too. He took good care of Mary and baby Jesus. It was God's plan.

The first Christmas night, God sent beautiful angels to tell the shepherds about his Son, Jesus.

"Glory to God in the highest!" sang the angels.

The shepherds were so surprised! Do you know what they did next?

The shepherds left their flocks of sheep out in the fields and came to Bethlehem to worship baby Jesus. The shepherds loved Jesus.

And did you know that Jesus came into this world for me too? He did. He really, really did.

Isn't that wonderful? Jesus came for ME.

Thank you, God, for giving us Christmas.

Happy birthday, Jesus!

Yes, I like everything about Christmas. But I think that the BEST thing is . . . Jesus came for ME!

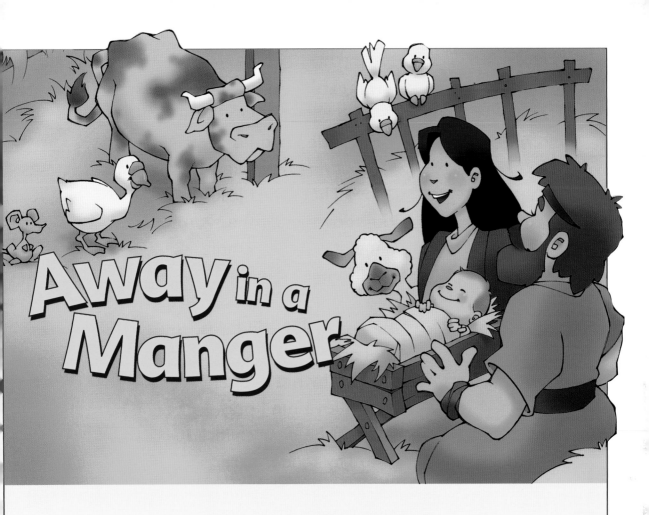

Away in a Manger

song lyrics by MARTIN LUTHER
illustrated by TERRY JULIEN

Away in a manger,
no crib for a bed,
The little Lord Jesus
laid down His sweet head;
The stars in the sky
looked down where He lay,
The little Lord Jesus,
asleep on the hay.

The cattle are lowing,
the baby awakes,
But little Lord Jesus,
no crying he makes.
I love Thee, Lord Jesus,
look down from the sky,
And stay by my cradle
till morning is nigh.

Be near me, Lord Jesus,
I ask Thee to stay
Close by me forever,
and love me I pray.
Bless all the dear children
in Thy tender care,
And take us to Heaven
to live with Thee there.

The BEST Thing About Easter

written by CHRISTINE HARDER TANGVALD
illustrated by KATHY COURI

Do you like Easter? I DO! I think Easter is FUN! I like to dye Easter eggs all different colors—pink ones, green ones, blue ones, orange ones, and yellow ones.

Which one is YOUR favorite?

Then after we dye the eggs . . . we HIDE them! I love to hunt for Easter eggs, don't you? How many can you find?

Yes, I think Easter eggs are fun! But Easter eggs aren't the BEST thing about Easter!

Sometimes we have CANDY Easter eggs with soft, squishy marshmallows on the inside. Sometimes we have gooey, chewy jelly beans that taste like lemon or cherry or peppermint! Yum, YUM, **YUM!** And sometimes we have dark chocolate Easter bunnies that melt in your mouth!

I like Easter candy . . . A LOT! But candy isn't the BEST thing about Easter.

Did you ever pet a soft, furry bunny at Easter time? I did—at my uncle's farm. I like soft, furry bunnies. Once my cousin got a fuzzy yellow duck that said, *"Quack, quack, quack!"* My other cousin got a cute baby chick that said, *"Peep, peep, peep!"*

I like furry bunnies and fuzzy ducks and cute baby chicks, don't you? But bunnies and ducks and chicks aren't the BEST thing about Easter.

Easter is in the springtime, and guess what happens then! I run, run, run on the green, green grass, UP the hill and DOWN the hill in the bright, warm sunshine. Whee!! Just WATCH me!

Everything is bursting with new life in the springtime. But springtime isn't the BEST thing about Easter.

I like to get ALL DRESSED UP on Easter Sunday, don't you? First I scrub, scrub, scrub in the tub and get all clean. Then I brush, brush, brush my hair. And then I put on my VERY BEST CLOTHES! Wow! Just look at me! I look terrific!

Then at church on Easter Sunday, we talk and laugh together. We sit and sing together, and we listen and pray together. We have a great time together too.

Oh, YES! I like getting all dressed up and being together on Easter Sunday. But even that isn't the BEST thing about Easter.

The very BEST THING about Easter is . . . **JESUS** . . . God's own Son!

Oh, yes! Jesus is the BEST THING about Easter.

You see, we have Easter because of Jesus.

Easter is about something wonderful that was part of God's AMAZING plan.

First a very sad thing happened. Jesus died on the cross.

But guess what! Jesus did not stay dead!

No, he did not! On the very first Easter morning, God made Jesus ALIVE again! The tomb where he was buried was EMPTY!

Jesus' friends were SO surprised and SO happy to see Jesus again. "Jesus is alive!" they said. "He is really alive!"

And then a little later, do you know what God did?

He took Jesus up, UP, **UP** . . . right through a cloud into HEAVEN! It was all part of GOD'S amazing plan!

But the MOST amazing part of God's plan is that Jesus died and lives again . . . for ME!

It's TRUE! Because Jesus loves me, you see. And he loves YOU too.

This is what love is: God loved us and sent His Son. 1 John 4:10

Oh yes! I like Easter eggs, and I like Easter candy, and I like soft furry bunnies and fuzzy baby ducks, and I like getting all dressed up and being together on Easter Sunday.

BUT . . . the BEST THING about Easter is Jesus! I'm GLAD Jesus loves me! I'm really, REALLY glad. Aren't you glad Jesus loves you too?

HAPPY EASTER, EVERYONE!

Jesus Lives!
The Easter Story

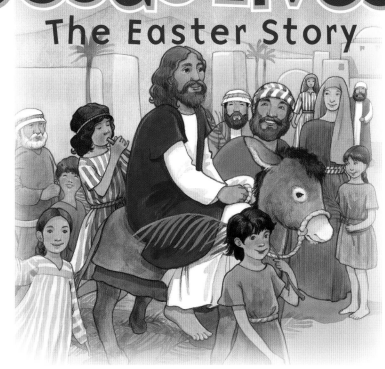

written by LAURA RING

illustrated by RONDA KRUM

"The king is coming!" the people shouted.

Soon Jesus came into the city of Jerusalem riding on a young donkey.

A large crowd gathered to see Jesus. "Hosanna in the highest!" the people shouted to Jesus. "Blessed is he who comes in the name of the Lord!"

Jesus and his disciples went to the upper room of a house in the city to celebrate Passover together. As the meal was being served, Jesus wrapped a towel around his waist.

He took a bowl of water and began washing the feet of all of his disciples. When he was finished, Jesus said, "Follow my example. You should serve others just as I serve you."

During the meal Jesus reminded the disciples that he would soon leave them. He took bread, gave thanks to God, broke it, and gave it to his disciples. He also took the cup, gave thanks, and gave it to his disciples.

Jesus said, "I'm giving this bread and cup to you. Remember me whenever you eat bread and drink from the cup together."

When they had finished the meal, they sang a song of worship to God and went to the Mount of Olives.

Jesus and his disciples went to a garden to pray. Jesus took Peter, James, and John with him and said, "My heart is heavy because I am so sad. Stay here with me."

Then Jesus went a little farther by himself and prayed to God, "Father, I will do whatever you want me to do."

Jesus prayed this prayer three times. Each time, he went back and found that his disciples were asleep because they were very tired. The third time Jesus woke them, saying, "Let's go! The one who will betray me is here!"

Judas Iscariot had been one of Jesus' friends. But now he came with men to arrest Jesus.

They took Jesus to the high priest to be judged. Some people were angry that Jesus said he was the Son of God. They didn't believe Jesus even though he only spoke the truth.

No one could find anything bad that Jesus had done. Even the governor, Pilate, wanted to set him free. But the crowds shouted, "Crucify him!" So Pilate turned Jesus over to the soldiers to be crucified.

Jesus was quiet. He knew this was part of his Father's plan.

The soldiers took Jesus away.

They dressed him like a king with a purple robe and a crown of thorns. They made fun of Jesus. They did not understand that the kingdom Jesus talked about was not like earthly kingdoms. It was the kingdom of God!

They led Jesus to a place called Golgotha. There they crucified the Son of God with two criminals, one on his right and one on his left.

But Jesus still loved the people. From the cross he said, "Father, forgive them. They do not know what they are doing."

Darkness came over the whole land. With his last breath, Jesus cried out, "Father, I put myself in your hands!" Then he died.

The earth shook and rocks split. The men who were guarding Jesus said, "He really was the Son of God!"

A rich man named Joseph was a follower of Jesus. He asked Pilate for Jesus' body so he could bury Jesus. Joseph placed Jesus' body in a new tomb and rolled a big stone in front of the entrance.

Some of the leaders of the people were afraid that Jesus' friends would come to take his body out of the tomb. So Pilate sent guards to the tomb to seal it and watch it.

At dawn on the first day of the week, Mary Magdalene and some women went to the tomb. They wanted to put spices on Jesus' body, as was the custom of their people.

But when the women arrived at the tomb, they were amazed! An angel of God had rolled the stone away and was sitting there. He was bright like a lightning flash and his clothes were as white as snow.

The angel said to the women, "Do not be afraid. Jesus is not here. He has risen just as he said. Jesus lives!"

The women were so happy that they ran to tell all Jesus' disciples what the angels said. The disciples were amazed. Could Jesus really be alive? YES! JESUS LIVES!

Jesus appeared to the women and to his other disciples many times. He wanted to show them that he was alive so that they could tell others.

He told them, "Go and tell all nations about me. Baptize them in the name of the Father, Son, and Holy Spirit. Teach them to obey everything I have told you. I promise I will always be with you."

The disciples believed Jesus and did what he said. They were filled with joy, knowing that . . . JESUS LIVES!

Let's Shine Jesus' Light on Halloween

written by
DIANE STORTZ

illustrated by
RUSTY FLETCHER

On Halloween I might see black cats, pointy hats, and creepy flying bats . . . But God's power is the reason I don't have to be afraid.

I have overcome the world. John 16:33

On Halloween I will help carve a pumpkin to make a jack-o-lantern with a toothy grin . . . But knowing God loves me is what really makes me smile.

How precious are your thoughts about me, O God! Psalm 139:17

On Halloween I will wear a costume and pretend to be my favorite cartoon character . . . But God knows everything about the real me.

You saw me before I was born. Every day of my life was recorded in your book. Psalm 139:16

On Halloween I will use a funny flashlight to help me see in the dark . . . But God's Word shows me how to live and which way to go every day.

Your word is a lamp for my feet and a light for my path. Psalm 119:105

On Halloween I will bring home a sack full of candy treats . . . But being friends with Jesus is sweeter than the yummiest chocolate bar.

This is my happy way of life: obeying your commandments. Psalm 119:56

Yes, Halloween is jack-o-lanterns, costumes, and candy on a dark and spooky night . . . But Jesus is the light of the world.

Jesus said to the people, 'I am the light of the world. If you follow me, you won't be stumbling through the darkness, because you will have the light that leads to life. John 8:12

Let's Celebrate God's Blessings on Thanksgiving

written by LISE CALDWELL
illustrated by PRISCILLA BURRIS

A very long time ago, the Pilgrims sailed to America where they could worship God as the Bible taught them.

A tribe of native people showed the Pilgrims how to plant crops that would grow in the new land.

After the harvest the Pilgrims held a special feast to thank God for their crop and for their new friends. On the first Thanksgiving, the Pilgrims asked their new friends to join them in a feast.

My family still celebrates Thanksgiving today!

At my house we invite my aunts and uncles and cousins for Thanksgiving dinner.

Open your homes to each other. 1 Peter 4:9

On the first Thanksgiving, 90 braves brought vegetables and hunted turkey and venison for the feast.

My grandmother brings a golden, crispy turkey to my house, and Aunt Debbie makes yummy sweet potatoes.

He gives food to every living creature. Psalm 136:25

On the first Thanksgiving, the Pilgrims thanked God for providing food and friends for them in their new home.

At my house my family holds hands around the table. We all tell God what we are thankful for—our home, our food, our family, and our friends.

Every good action and perfect gift is from God. James 1:17

On the first Thanksgiving, everyone played games together. The braves had bow and arrow contests, and the Pilgrims shot their muskets. They even ran races.

At my house we play games too! Uncle Greg organizes a game of flag football in the yard. When it gets dark, we go inside and play charades.

He gives us everything to enjoy. 1 Timothy 6:17

Even after the first Thanksgiving, the Pilgrims kept thanking and praising God for bringing them to a new land where they were free to worship.

At my house we thank God every day for giving us food and homes and family, and a country where we are free to worship him!

Thank the Lord because he is good. Psalm 106:1

Happy Thanksgiving!